ROMANCE

Often derided as an inferior form of literature, "romance" as a literary mode or genre defies satisfactory definition, dividing critics, scholars and readers alike.

In this lucid, imaginative guidebook, Barbara Fuchs:

- traces the myriad transformations of romance throughout literary history
- examines the concept's relation to larger questions of literary and cultural theory
- asks what the history of romance can tell us about the theories of genre
- probes the resistance to romance, asking what broader issues might be in play
- explores definitions which might help us to recognize and analyze it in new forms
- argues the usefulness of romance to critics as a literary strategy rather than a fixed genre

Romance is a clear and wide-ranging introduction for students of literary history, comparative literature and modern literary forms. It is also a convincing case for a literary concept too often set to one side.

Barbara Fuchs is Associate Professor of Romance Languages at the University of Pennsylvania. She is the author of *Passing for Spain: Cervantes and the Fictions of Identity* (2003), and *Mimesis and Empire: The New World, Islam, and European Identities* (2001).

THE NEW CRITICAL IDIOM

SERIES EDITOR: JOHN DRAKAKIS, UNIVERSITY OF STIRLING

The New Critical Idiom is an invaluable series of introductory guides to today's critical terminology. Each book:

- provides a handy, explanatory guide to the use (and abuse) of the term
- offers an original and distinctive overview by a leading literary and cultural critic
- relates the term to the larger field of cultural representation.

With a strong emphasis on clarity, lively debate, and the widest possible breadth of examples, *The New Critical Idiom* is an indispensable approach to key topics in literary studies.

Also available in this series:

ROMANCE

Barbara Fuchs

Routledge
Taylor & Francis Group

NEW YORK AND LONDON

First published 2004
by Routledge
270 Madison Ave, New York, NY 10016

Simultaneously published in the UK
by Routledge
2 Park Square, Milton Park, Abingdon, Oxon OX14 4RN

Routledge is an imprint of the Taylor & Francis Group

© 2004 Barbara Fuchs

Typeset in Adobe Garamond and Scala Sans by
Keystroke, Jacaranda Lodge, Wolverhampton
Printed and bound in Great Britain by
TJ International Ltd, Padstow, Cornwall

Library of Congress Cataloging in Publication Data
Fuchs, Barbara, 1970–
     Romance / Barbara Fuchs.
          p. cm. – (New critical idiom)
     Includes bibliographical references and index.
     1. Romances–History and criticism.   2. Literature,
     Medieval–History and criticism.   3. European literature–
     Renaissance, 1450–1600–History and criticism.   I. Title.
     II. Series.
     PN56 .R6F83   2004
     809.3—dc22   2004003902

British Library Cataloguing in Publication Data
A catalogue record for this book is available from the British Library

ISBN 0–415–21260–x (Hbk)
ISBN 0–415–21261–8 (Pbk)

Para Todd, ¿quién más?

Contents

SERIES EDITOR'S PREFACE

The New Critical Idiom is a series of introductory books which seeks to extend the lexicon of literary terms, in order to address the radical changes which have taken place in the study of literature during the last decades of the twentieth century. The aim is to provide clear, well-illustrated accounts of the full range of terminology currently in use, and to evolve histories of its changing usage.

The current state of the discipline of literary studies is one where there is considerable debate concerning basic questions of terminology. This involves, among other things, the boundaries which distinguish the literary from the non-literary; the position of literature within the larger sphere of culture; the relationship between literatures of different cultures; and questions concerning the relation of literary to other cultural forms within the context of interdisciplinary studies.

It is clear that the field of literary criticism and theory is a dynamic and heterogeneous one. The present need is for individual volumes on terms which combine clarity of exposition with an adventurousness of perspective and a breadth of application. Each volume will contain as part of its apparatus some indication of the direction in which the definition of particular terms is likely to move, as well as expanding the disciplinary boundaries within which some of these terms have been traditionally contained. This will involve some re-situation of terms within the larger field of cultural representation, and will introduce examples from the area of film and the modern media in addition to examples from a variety of literary texts.

ACKNOWLEDGMENTS

The process of producing a volume on romance is almost fated to be dilatory and meandering. I would like to thank all the friends and colleagues who patiently encouraged me on the wandering paths of romance. At Routledge, John Drakakis and Liz Thompson kindly supported my protracted efforts. My research assistants, Brooke Stafford and Madera Allan, eased my unwieldy transition between libraries and pulled off marvels of their own. Catherine Connors kindly read an early chapter. David Baker, Rita Copeland, Catherine Sanok, and Emily Steiner lent their invaluable expertise to several sections. Marina Brownlee shared with me her broad comparative understanding of romance and graciously read the entire manuscript. I owe special thanks to Patricia Parker, who first proposed the project and whose own work on romance has served as constant inspiration. Marshall Brown, whose critical and editorial acuity are matched only by his generosity, read versions early and late, providing unfailing support. This book is dedicated to Todd Lynch, for his understanding, his unwavering encouragement, and his willingness to help me delve into romance.

INTRODUCTION

Romances are generally composed of the Constant Loves and invincible Courages of Hero's, Heroins, Kings and Queens, Mortals of the first Rank, and so forth; where lofty Language, miraculous Contingencies and impossible Performances, elevate and surprize the Reader into a giddy Delight which leaves him flat upon the Ground whenever he gives of, and vexes him to think how he has suffer'd himself to be pleased and transported, concern'd and afflicted at the several Passages which he has Read, *viz.* these Knights Success to their Damosels Misfortunes, and such like, when he is forced to be very well convinced that 'tis all a lye.

William Congreve, "Preface to *Incognita*, 1691"

"Romance" is most often used in literary studies to allude to forms conveying literary pleasure the critic thinks readers would be better off without.

Margaret Doody, *The True Story of the Novel*, 15

Romance is a notoriously slippery category. Critics disagree about whether it is a genre or a mode, about its origins and history, even about what it encompasses. Yet, paradoxically, readers are often able to identify romance almost tacitly: they know it when they see it. My students call it "that fairy-tale feeling," a mixture of the archaic and the idealizing, much like the ingredients that the Restoration dramatist William Congreve identifies above. As Doody reminds us, however, despite this accessibility or perhaps precisely because of it romance has often been singled out for censure as an unworthy form of literature.

This volume charts the multiple, protean transformations of romance throughout literary history. Instead of settling on a single definition in the hope of capturing romance in its original shape, it demonstrates how different conceptions of the term emerge dynamically, in opposition to other types of literary production. Moreover, it argues that romance, as a critical idiom, may be most useful to contemporary readers if it retains some of its historical commodiousness and is conceptualized as a set of literary strategies that can be adopted by different forms. Thus, although the chapters that follow focus on texts that have been generically identified as romances, however controversially, in different periods of literary history, they simultaneously present an understanding of romance as strategy. Focusing on what romance does and enables within a narrative not only reveals its bones, but shows most clearly how it appears within a variety of genres. The dialectical movement between the many kinds of romance as genre and romance as strategy affords the fullest sense of the term. While no one book could encompass all the manifestations and varieties of romance, the following chapters aim to provide a broad theoretical and historical survey of its multiple incarnations.

Precisely because the history of romance is so complex, the term serves as a touchstone for larger questions of literary and cultural theory. By exploring various definitions of romance, readers may find ways to conceptualize broader problems of genre, reception, and the political import of imaginative literature. To this end, this volume considers the following questions: How does the history of romance as a category force us to rethink the historicization of literary forms? What kind of definition can we provide for our own time that is both historically situated and yet flexible enough to help us recognize and analyze new forms of romance? Also, how do reactions to romance register cultural attitudes towards the marvelous or to narratives with a broad popular appeal? To what extent is the resistance to romance a resistance to the imaginative force of literature, or to readerly pleasure?

DEFINITIONS

The definition of romance in the *Oxford English Dictionary* (OED) reads a little like Borges' fable of the Chinese encyclopedia, with categories that range from the minute to the universal and which are often mutually exclusive.

Here is an abridged version, limited to definitions relevant to our purposes:

Romance:

> I. 1. The vernacular language of France, as opposed to Latin. In later use also extended to related forms of speech, as Provençal and Spanish, and now commonly used as a generic or collective name for the whole group of languages descended from Latin.

> II. 2. A tale in verse, embodying the adventures of some hero of chivalry, esp. of those of the great cycles of medieval legend, and belonging both in matter and form to the ages of knighthood; also, in later use, a prose tale of a similar character.
> Orig. denoting a composition in the vernacular (French, etc.), as contrasted with works in Latin.

> 3. A fictitious narrative in prose of which the scene and incidents are very remote from those of ordinary life; esp. one of the class prevalent in the 16th and 17th centuries, in which the story is often overlaid with long disquisitions and digressions. Also occas., a long poem of a similar type. The immediate source of this use was app. F. roman.

> b. A romantic novel or narrative.

> 4. A Spanish historical ballad or short poem of a certain form.
> From Sp. romance, whence also F. romance. Attributive uses, as romance-book, -verse, etc., are common in works on Spanish literature.

> 5. That class of literature which consists of romances; romantic fiction. spec. a love story; that class of literature which consists of love stories.

> b. Romantic or imaginative character or quality; redolence or suggestion of, association with, the adventurous and chivalrous. spec. a love affair; idealistic character or quality in a love affair.

> 6. An extravagant fiction, invention, or story; a wild or wanton exaggeration; a picturesque falsehood.

The definition ranges from the linguistic to the literary, and eventually escapes the realm of language altogether, to settle on what is perhaps the most frequent meaning of the word in common parlance: a love affair.

While all these meanings are important for literary notions of romance, the critical idiom needs to be disentangled from other definitions. The term that I will discuss is not specific to the romance languages; in fact, as we will see, the cognate terms for "romance" in those languages have very different meanings. Neither is the term historically specific: although critics working in different fields and national traditions might argue that theirs is the true or original romance, the force of the term comes precisely from its transformations and reiterations over time. Nor is literary romance necessarily concerned with eros, although this popular sense of the term often permeates it. Finally, literary romance must be distinguished from the category of the *Romantic*, which describes a specific period in literary history (and is the subject of another volume in this series).

GENRE, MODE, STRATEGY

In the narrow literary sense, *romance* is the name given to a particular *genre*: the narrative poems that emerge in twelfth-century France and quickly make their way around Europe (as in OED II.2). These popular poems were known as romances because they were written in the vernacular, or *romance*, languages derived from Latin (OED I.1), as opposed to Latin itself, which was the traditional language of learning. These poems are typically concerned with aristocratic characters such as kings and queens, knights and ladies, and their chivalric pursuits. They are often organized around a quest, whether for love or adventure, and involve a variety of marvelous elements. This is the genre from which we derive our popular sense of romance, as in the epigraph above.

But this more restricted definition of romance quickly becomes problematic, as we realize that the thematic preoccupations of the genre, and at least some of its formal characteristics, continue to make their appearance throughout Europe for many centuries. The term is variously applied to everything from Spenser's *The Faerie Queene*, to Shakespeare's late plays, to seventeenth-century French classicizing fictions, to Harlequin romances. Moreover, medieval romance reaches back in time as well as projecting forward: many of the twelfth-century romances take their plots from much earlier stories, and seem as closely related to prior literatures in their subject-matter as to each other in their form.

The tendency for certain characteristics of the medieval chivalric form to overflow its specific limits has led some critics to propose a different, much broader notion of romance, one that transcends the specificities of genre and can be variously applied to verse or prose texts in a variety of historical settings. The most influential exponent of this sense of romance in the twentieth century was the structuralist critic Northrop Frye, who described romance as one of the central *modes* of literature in two seminal studies, *Anatomy of Criticism* (1957) and *The Secular Scripture: A Study of the Structure of Romance* (1976).

Frye follows Aristotle to suggest that fiction may be classified "by the hero's power of action, which may be greater than ours, less, or roughly the same" (Frye 1957: 33). Romance is one of the modes that features a superior hero:

> If superior in *degree* to other men and to his environment, the hero is the typical hero of romance, whose actions are marvelous but who is himself identified as a human being. The hero of romance moves in a world in which the ordinary laws of nature are slightly suspended: prodigies of courage and endurance, unnatural to us, are natural to him, and enchanted weapons, talking animals, terrifying ogres and witches, and talismans of miraculous power violate no rule of probability once the postulates of romance have been established.
>
> (Frye 1957: 33)

This definition focuses on the hero to the exclusion of other elements (begging, for example, the question of the *heroine*), and leaves much unspecified. It also threatens to set romance apart from other kinds of literary production, as though the category were impermeable and self-sufficient. Despite these problems, however, it usefully expands romance from a particular genre into a more general type of literary production.

Frye is also interested in the meaning of romance (what Fredric Jameson calls the semantic, rather than the syntactic, register [1975: 136]) as a *mythos* or archetype, a kind of universal paradigm for fiction. Frye's mythos of romance involves a series of adventures, collectively labelled the *quest*, that pits the hero against his antagonist in a simple, dialectical structure. As Jameson points out, romance is organized around the conceptual opposition between good and evil (Jameson 1975: 140). Characters are generally for or against the quest in a straightforward fashion, although of course the villains may practice deceit. A general example of this archetypal plot is the story of the hero who kills the dragon or sea-monster that terrorizes a kingdom, and then marries the king's daughter (Frye 1957: 186–9). Perhaps one of the most famous versions of this plot in English literature is the story of the Redcrosse Knight (aka St. George) and his fight against the apocalyptic dragon who terrorizes Eden in Book I of Edmund Spenser's *The Faerie Queene* (1591, 1596).

The presentation of these archetypes in romance, Frye suggests, is characterized by idealization and wish-fulfillment: the projection of the social ideals of a ruling class onto literary heroes and heroines. Thus romance generally involves aristocratic protagonists, or ones who are miraculously revealed as such after living a lower-class existence, in a kind of "blood will tell" move in which social status is ultimately disclosed. Romance also generally upholds such normative values as fealty and chastity, although not always in an uncomplicated fashion. While Frye himself is not particularly interested in political readings of romance, he describes its engagement with dominant ideologies as the "kidnapping" of romance in order to "reflect certain ascendant religious or social ideals" (Frye 1976: 29–30). Conversely, Frye notes, romance is often marked by a persistent nostalgia for some other time (or, one might add, place) that undermines the social ideals of the here and now. The idealization of romance is often achieved through a nostalgic purchase on the past. Romance values the antique and the exotic, and expresses a powerful longing for what came before,

> In fable or romance of Uther's son
> Begirt with British and Armoric knights;
> And all who since, baptized or infidel
> Jousted in Aspramont or Montalban,
> Damasco, or Marocco, or Trebisond,
> Or whom Biserta sent from Afric shore

When Charlemagne with all his peerage fell
By Fontarabbia.
                    (Milton, *Paradise Lost*, I. 580–8)

The nostalgic evocation of other times and places, complete with exotic nomenclature, as in the passage above, challenges our understanding of romance as a socially conservative form. Through the lens of nostalgia, the past can pose a significant challenge to the present. This sense of romance as an alternative to contemporary reality proved very powerful for the Romantics, in the early years of the nineteenth century, when the return to an idealized past was perceived as a reprieve from the cultural ravages of industrialization.

Part of the problem with Frye's notion of a romance mode is that it relies very heavily on an archetypal idea of literature, according to which all texts fall into one category or another, and exhibit certain inherent characteristics. This works less well when we attempt to describe hybrid texts, or those which seem to include moments of romance without existing fully in the "mode." One challenge when defining the critical idiom thus involves accounting for romance as one aspect of a text, rather than simply the category into which the whole will fit.

Frye also necessarily subsumes the differences among texts to his interest in identifying a continuity or tradition. Jameson notes that although Frye's approach does not limit romance to one historical moment, it tends to erase the markers of history and to make romance self-identical over the course of time (Jameson 1975: 155–6). Jameson, as a historical materialist, is more interested in accounting for the form that romance takes in specific historical and ideological contexts. He reads medieval romance, for example, as a response to the "emergent class solidarity" of the feudal nobility: the knight who appears evil by virtue of his unknowability and oppositional stance is eventually revealed as a version of the self, while evil is projected onto an otherworldly realm of magic (Jameson 1975: 161). This understanding, as I discuss in Chapter 3, has been refined and challenged by medievalists who have attended to the specific and local historical contexts of individual romances.

In more general terms, Jameson recalls for us the importance of envisioning the history of romance as a reflection of particular ideological contexts:

> A history of romance as a mode becomes possible, in other words, when we project it as a history of the various codes which, in the increasingly secularized and rational world that emerges from the collapse of feudalism, are called upon to assume the literary function of those older codes which have now become so many dead languages. Or, to put it the other way round, the fate of romance as a form is dependent on the availability of elements more acceptable to the reader than those older magical categories for which some adequate substitute must be invented.
>
> (Jameson 1975: 142–3)

Jameson's inquiry is thus concerned with tracing the function of romance in a particular time and place, as well as with charting how romance is updated to fit the changing "codes" of its culture.

Although Jameson never makes it explicit, Frye's notion of the "kidnapped romance" animates his investigation; what for Frye is a deformation or deviation from romance's enduring nature is for Jameson the whole point of an inquiry into mode or genre. For our purposes, it is important to recognize that romance, like many other literary forms, is allusive and self-referential, constantly harking back to a literary and cultural tradition, while also highly adaptable to particular historical and ideological contexts.

Post-structuralist theory invites us to consider romance in terms of what it performs as opposed to what it is. Thus Patricia Parker's reading of romance focuses on what it *does* and *undoes* within texts. One of Parker's central contributions is to recognize that romance can appear within texts that are not necessarily in a romance genre or mode. Parker reads romance primarily as an undoing or complication of narrative progression in texts that range from epic to lyric. In this view, romance is "a form that simultaneously quests for and postpones a particular end, objective, or object" (Parker 1979: 4). Resolution becomes elusive, and identity fraught, in texts characterized by "the connection between naming, identity, and closure or ending" (Parker 1979: 5). Parker is interested more in the dilation and error of romance, in the ways that it interferes with the teleological progress of the narrative, than in the quest itself: "For poets for whom the attainment of an end is problematic, or impossible, the focus may be less on arrival or completion than on the strategy of delay" (Parker 1979: 5).

For purposes of this discussion, I would like to adapt Frye and Parker's contributions to consider romance as a literary and textual *strategy*. Under this definition, the term describes a concatenation of both narratological elements and literary topoi, including idealization, the marvelous, narrative delay, wandering, and obscured identity, that, as Parker suggests, both pose a quest and complicate it. I find this the most useful notion of romance because it accounts for the greatest number of instances, allowing us to address the occurrence of romance within texts that are clearly classified as some other genre and incorporating the hybridization and malleability that, as we shall see, are such key elements of romance. The instrumental notion of romance as a recurrent textual strategy allows us to recognize its many manifestations and transformations throughout literary history; it may well be our best chance to capture its protean nature, as well as to address the broadest definitions of the term. But it also allows us to deconstruct the many oppositions set up by literary history, such as romance versus epic or romance versus novel. These become more complicated once we identify the presence of romance within its ostensible opposites.

ENGLISH ONLY?

Part of the problem with defining romance as I have endeavored to do above is that while critics may apply the term to literature in a variety of languages, those languages do not have a word for this sense of romance. *Roman* in French or German now means simply *novel*, as does *romanzo* in Italian. *Romance* in Spanish is a short ballad form (OED 4A). Conversely, when Spanish critics wish to refer to the sense of romance that I have been discussing, they call it *lo novelesco*. This peculiar situation has led some critics to challenge the very term romance as outdated or limited by the constraints of a particular critical tradition.

Margaret Doody argues that critics working in the Anglo-American academy essentially invented the distinction between novel and romance in order to imagine an English origin for what was a much older form (Doody 1996). In this schema, she argues, literary theory adopts as its gold standard the notion of progress towards realism: "The Novel replaces the Romance as Reason replaces Superstition, and as the Model-T Ford replaces the horse and carriage" (Doody 1996: 3). Doody is interested in tracing a longer history for the novel while avoiding progressive or teleological models. To this end, she proclaims: "Romance and the Novel are one. The separation between them is part of a problem, not part of a solution" (Doody 1996: 15).

Rather than rethinking the hierarchy or the terms of the classification, Doody discards the category of romance altogether. This seems a case of throwing the baby out with the bath-water. The applicability and usefulness of the notion of romance we have sketched out transcend the particular myth of literary history exposed by Doody. Yet any critical definition that takes her important argument into account must present romance as something other than a bad alternative or insufficient predecessor to the novel. In fact, we can avoid the progress narrative altogether by turning to an instrumental understanding of romance as a literary strategy that appears in a variety of genres, as I have suggested above. This redefinition accounts for the self-conscious use of romance by authors working within a variety of traditions, and accommodates romance as one of the many voices within the novel, instead of its poor cousin.

This study gives a sense of the place of romance within several national traditions. Romance does not, as we shall see, respect those boundaries, and this approach allows us to move beyond the Anglo-American paradigm identified by Doody. Because I have consistently aimed for the broadest possible definition of romance in the European tradition, however, I will necessarily focus on central moments in this tradition instead of providing anything like a comprehensive history. Even so, it is important to bear in mind that romance relies heavily on allusion and reflexivity, and that it is necessary to trace the historical change in romance as well as its continuity.

In addition to addressing the occurrence of romance in various times and places, this book foregrounds the vexed treatment of romance in literary history. For romance, especially in the instrumental sense I have adopted here, is often defined relatively rather than absolutely, and retrospectively rather than contemporaneously. That is, texts are read as romance primarily in relation or comparison to other texts – as in the opposition between epic and romance – or in order to distinguish them from their successors – as in the distinction between romance and novel.

The frequent controversies over romance that involve questions of definition and scope, and of its value for readers, may, I conjecture, teach us as much about the dynamics of literary theory and history as about romance itself.

1

CLASSICAL ROMANCE

We often use Greek terms and definitions such as tragedy, epic, lyric, to describe texts composed much later, yet for the fictional narratives of the classical world we are forced to rely on more modern terms, retrospectively applied. Discussing romance in Greek and Latin texts, that is, entails bringing to bear much later categories on earlier texts. Antiquity never theorized romance; in fact, much of the neglect that classical romance suffered in scholarship until very recently had to do with the theoretical vacuum where fictional narratives were concerned.

The Greeks had terms for different aspects of these texts: *plasma* (fictitious creation), *drama* (story of action), *diēgēma* (narrative), *historia* (account of what has been discovered), but no overarching category like *novel* (Reardon 1991: 7). Critics have speculated that this critical neglect reflects the low regard in which these fictions were held, despite their presumed appeal to a popular audience (Perry 1967: 4–5). Although critics have traced the connections between the prose fiction of antiquity and such genres as biography, travel literature, and historiography, they generally agree that there was no classification of fictional narratives as a particular genre. In analyzing classical romance, as we will do here, we are therefore necessarily working with categories that would never have been applied by authors, readers, or critics at the time the texts were produced. Yet these categories are hardly arbitrary; in some ways, they have structured our modern understanding of literary history. As subsequent chapters will show, central distinctions such as that between epic and romance organize our understanding of texts from the Renaissance onwards.

The opposition between epic and romance, explored most recently by David Quint, is perhaps most clearly visible in Virgil's *Aeneid* (29–19 BC) the story of the Trojan Aeneas' foundation of Rome. Virgil juxtaposes Homer's *Odyssey* and *Iliad* in his poem, sharpening the distinctions between these predecessors and exacerbating the ideological implications of their form. Aeneas is nearly derailed from his fated mission by a series of Odyssean adventures, and most seriously by the amorous welcome he receives in Africa from Dido, Queen of Carthage. The Iliadic portion of the poem finally takes Aeneas to Italy, where, after much bloodshed, he will found the Roman nation. It is through the lens of the *Aeneid* that we read epic as an account of warfare leading to the birth of a nation, focused on a martial hero who represents the group. In this context, romance appears instead as a detour or wandering from the teleological thrust of epic, characterized by circularity or stasis and by the seductions of eros and individual adventures.

In order to understand this foundational opposition, this chapter first analyzes the romance strategies of Homer's *Odyssey* (750–700 BC), which one critic calls the "fountainhead" of romance (Reardon 1991: 6). It then surveys the texts that fall under the category of "Greek romance" in the generic sense, and examines the controversies over that classification. At the same time, it charts a broader, alternative understanding of romance as literary strategy in the classical world and touches briefly on some of the many texts that exemplify romance in this sense.

ODYSSEAN WANDERINGS

> Keep Ithaka always in your mind.
> Arriving there is what you are destined for.
> But do not hurry the journey at all.
> Better if it lasts for years,
> so you are old by the time you reach the island,
> wealthy with all you have gained on the way,
> not expecting Ithaka to make you rich.
>   C.P. Cavafy, "Ithaka"

Homer's poem on the hero Odysseus' return (*nostos*) to Ithaca and his wife Penelope after the Trojan War establishes some of the most enduring and recurring of romance strategies. While the *Odyssey* shares the overall epic form of the *Iliad*, it is focused on a very different set of issues. This is not a poem about war but about the vexed return home. It is concerned far more with the individual hero and his transformations than with any corporate goal. The interest of the narrative lies precisely in the obstacles and detours in Odysseus' way; that is, in the romance that delays his progress while advancing the text.

The urgency of the return is determined by the dire straits in which Penelope and Telemachus find themselves. After twenty years of Odysseus' absence, Penelope is being aggressively courted by suitors who, while they wait for her favor, make free with Odysseus' possessions and consume his wealth. As the suitors become increasingly impatient, Penelope despairs of being able to hold them off any longer. Meanwhile, Odysseus, unwillingly detained by the nymph Calypso on her island, longs for home. (Author's note: For all Greek names, such as Calypso, I have chosen the spelling most commonly encountered in subsequent literary texts in English. I have silently modified the spelling in translations to conform with this principle.) When the goddess Athena finally arranges his release, he is thwarted once again by the vengeful Poseidon and shipwrecked on the coast of the Phaiakians, who, from his first encounter with the princess Nausicaa, receive him kindly. In an extensive narrative detour, Odysseus relates to them his previous adventures, from the aftermath of the victory at Troy to the loss of his men and his sojourn with Calypso. The Phaiakians provide him with a ship and he finally returns to Ithaca, where he must face the challenge of the suitors, grown ever more arrogant in his continued absence.

In a sense, the poem itself opens with a detour. A brief council of the gods serves as exposition, establishing Athena's concern for Odysseus and giving us the basic rudiments of the plot. The scene then moves to Ithaca with the goddess. Instead of Odysseus, we first meet his son, Telemachus, as we follow him on his search for news of his father, a miniature quest in its own right. This embedded narrative of Telemachus' wanderings heightens readerly expectations, providing an oblique introduction to the hero – we hear much about Odysseus before we finally encounter him – and foreshadowing the voyages and encounters of the main plot.

Telemachus travels to the wondrous court of Menelaos, Helen's husband, who describes his own difficult return from Troy to Greece. Although Menelaos has recovered Helen, and acquired a great treasure on his wanderings, his life is marred by melancholy:

> How painfully I wandered
> before I brought it home! Seven years at sea,
> Kypros, Phoinikia, Egypt, and still farther
> among the sun-burnt races. . . .
> How gladly I should live one third as rich
> to have my friends back safe at home! – my friends
> who died on Troy's wide seaboard, far
> from the grazing lands of Argos.
> But as things are, nothing but grief is left me
> for those companions.
>
> (Homer 1998: 4.87–111)

(Author's note: Because this translation is so widely used in English-language contexts, I have given Fitzgerald's line numbering for the verse instead of the original's.)

Menelaos' wanderings to the far confines of the Greek world on his roundabout route home anticipate the marvelous travels of Odysseus. Yet Menelaos, who has managed to return home, is paradoxically full of nostalgia (from *nostos*, return and *algos*, suffering) for Troy. So powerful is the yearning for the past that it colors Menelaos' life, even among the splendor of his possessions. Such longing pervades the poem, and this early episode complicates the possibility of resolution to so much wandering desire. The strategy that we see here in the *Odyssey* comes to be one of the primary features of romance: the dilation or postponement of the object of desire rather than its achievement.

Odysseus himself is introduced as the object of Menelaos' longing:

> And there is one I miss more than the other
> dead I mourn for; sleep and food alike
> grow hateful when I think of him. No soldier
> took on so much, went through so much, as Odysseus.
> That seems to have been his destiny, and this mine –

> to feel each day the emptiness of his absence,
> ignorant, even, whether he lived or died.
>
> > (Homer 1998: 4.114–20)

This is different from Penelope or Telemachus' longing for Odysseus, but equally powerful. Before introducing Odysseus on his own quest for Ithaca, the poet renders him as an absence experienced from multiple perspectives, a man missed by a vulnerable wife, a diffident son, a melancholy comrade-in-arms. This perspectivism is literalized in the figure of the shape-shifting Proteus, the Ancient of the Sea, who must be forced to retain his shape before he can provide Menelaos with news of Odysseus. His mutability and slipperiness make Proteus a powerful symbol for romance transformations. Menelaos tricks Proteus with his own shape-shifting, disguising himself in the skin of a seal (Homer 1998: 4.469–79), a ruse which anticipates both Odysseus' escape from the Cyclops and the enchantress Circe's actual transformation of his men into beasts.

In a heavily ironic moment, Menelaos recalls also how Helen, "drawn by some superhuman power" (Homer 1998: 4.296), had tried to undo the Greeks in Troy by playing on their nostalgia as they lay in hiding inside the famous wooden horse, itself another animal disguise of sorts:

> Three times you walked around it, patting it everywhere,
> and called by name the flower of our fighters,
> making your voice sound like their wives, calling.
>
> > (Homer 1998: 4.299–301)

This key passage connects the generalized longing of Menelaos' court with a much more dangerous and deliberate use of desire against military might. It sets up some of the central oppositions that animate romance as a counter-strategy to epic progress or achievement. Desire, whether associated with Helen's voice, here prefiguring the sirens, or with the warriors' actual longing for their wives, has the potential to sabotage heroic exploits. It is only Odysseus' own intervention, as he forcibly silences a comrade, that safeguards the stratagem of the wooden horse.

As this brief recollection of Helen's duplicity suggests, romance associates female figures in particular with both treacherousness and erotic enchantment. These characters – nymphs, sirens, witches – are ultimately linked with a kind of stasis that contravenes the quest, which is typically gendered male. As such, they occupy a central role in Odysseus' story of his travels and travails. When we finally encounter our hero, in Book 5, he is trapped by the nymph Calypso. This is a sweet captivity, to be sure: the nymph offers him all kinds of blandishments and even immortality, yet Odysseus longs to escape:

> The sweet days of his life time
> were running out in anguish over his exile,
> for long ago the nymph had ceased to please.
> Though he fought shy of her and her desire,
> he lay with her each night, for she compelled him.
> But when the day came he sat on the rocky shore
> and broke his own heart groaning, with eyes wet
> scanning the bare horizon of the sea.
>
> (Homer 1998: 5.159–66)

It requires divine intervention to free Odysseus from his thralldom, in the form of Hermes, the messenger god, sent by Zeus to compel Calypso to free him. This intervention *contra* romance becomes a hallmark of the tension between epic and romance in the classical tradition and its Renaissance avatars. The "descent from heaven" motif serves as a literal *deus ex machina* who releases the hero from romance enchantment (Greene 1963).

The release of the hero will be a central turning point in Virgil's recreation of the *Odyssey* in the first half of the *Aeneid*. Aeneas relates his own Odyssean adventures to the sympathetic Dido, Queen of Carthage, who offers him solace and sustenance after he is shipwrecked on her coast. Unlike Odysseus, Aeneas is not trapped by Dido: he has simply become too fond of her and her city, and forgetful of his duty to found Rome. In a crucial reformulation of the *Odyssey*, eros here obstructs not the hero's return from past martial exploits, but his readiness or availability for future combat. Virgil's echo of the *Odyssey* in Mercury's descent to admonish Aeneas to move on cements the tradition of romance derailing epic, and maps a series of patriarchal and imperial oppositions onto the narrative forms: female versus male, East versus West, chaos versus order, nature versus reason (Quint 1993: 24–31). Dido accuses Aeneas of heartlessness and worse: "Liar and cheat! Some rough Caucasian cliff/ Begot you on flint. Hyrcanian tigresses/ Tendered their teats to you" (Virgil 1984: 505–7). Aeneas, the narrator curtly tells us, is "duty-bound" (545). In a literary tradition deeply influenced by the *Aeneid*, the opposition of eros, associated with romance, and war, associated with epic, develops into a major theme. Thus, by contradistinction, romance becomes an alternative to teleology and historical destiny (Quint 1993: 9).

The fabulous world of Odysseus' travels already limns some of these oppositions, albeit in a less rigid fashion. When Odysseus relates his travels to the Phaiakians, he recalls a number of perils gendered female that threatened to derail him: the monsters Scylla and Charibdis, between whom it is impossible to pass unscathed, the sirens whose songs bewitch sailors (in a reference back to Menelaos' nostalgia, the sirens choose a "song of Troy" to lure Odysseus and his men [Homer 1998: 12.234]). Yet although the geography of the monstrous and marvelous is closely associated with the feminine, the episode of the Cyclops, perhaps the most frightening of them all, is gendered male throughout. In this bloody encounter based on folk narratives, Odysseus uses his guile to trick the savage monster, who is a creature without law or civility. He tells Polyphemus that his name is "Nohbdy," then plies him with wine until the monster is too drunk to defend himself. Then Odysseus puts out his single eye with a sharpened stake, confident that the monster's cries for help will be ignored when he bellows "Nohbdy, Nohbdy's tricked me, Nohbdy's ruined me!" (Homer 1998: 9.444).

Perhaps the most dangerous version of feminine stasis occurs on the island of the enchantress Circe, "dire beauty and divine" (Homer 1998: 10.150) who turns men into beasts:

> Low she sang
> in her beguiling voice, while on her loom
> she wove ambrosial fabric sheer and bright,
> by that craft known to the goddesses of heaven. . . .
> On thrones she seated them, and lounging chairs,
> while she prepared a meal of cheese and barley
> and amber honey mixed with Pramnian wine,
> adding her own vile pinch, to make them lose
> desire or thought of our dear father land.

Scarce had they drunk when she flew after them
with her long stick and shut them in a pigsty –
bodies, voices, heads, and bristles, all
swinish now, though minds were still unchanged.

(Homer 1998: 10.243–65)

The transformation wrought by Circe has been variously glossed as the revelation of the primitive nature that lies beneath a civilized veneer, or of those primal urges of appetite and sexuality that link us to animals. Strikingly, one of the ingredients in Circe's brew is forgetfulness, the opposite of the nostalgia that animates the poem. If the enchantress had her way, these sailors would never return home. But Odysseus extracts a promise from Circe that she will do him no harm if he becomes her lover, and then persuades her to restore his men to their original shapes. Yet once restored they merely linger in Circe's house, feasting the months away. The implication is that this kind of enchantment, though appearing more benign, is as dangerous as the more overt sorcery. Odysseus' shipmates insist on the need to proceed:

Captain, shake off this trance, and think of home –
if home indeed awaits us,

if we shall ever see
your own well-timbered hall on Ithaca.

(Homer 1998: 10.521–4)

What is at stake is the very shape of the story: Odysseus cannot simply decide that Circe or Calypso will do very well, thank you; if the narrative is to continue he must return to his original quest for Ithaca and Penelope. We might thus think of romance as composed of the tension between these two movements: the quest, and the constant delays or detours from that quest. The narrative thrust of romance is constantly undone by narrative suspension, yet the latter sustains the story even as it postpones resolution.

Although female characters are often associated with stasis, it would be overly simplistic to equate the feminine with delay, the masculine with progress. Even within the Circe episode, there is the telling instance of Elpenor, who is forever prevented from returning home when he takes a drunken fall to his death from the enchantress' roof. (The figure of the man undone by his own appetites reappears in Spenser's treatment of the Circe theme in Book 3 of *The Faerie Queene* as the stubborn Grille, who refuses to be restored to humanity.) More importantly, the threat of stasis appears at times without being associated with a specific gender, as in the episode of the Lotus Eaters, an entire people devoted to oblivion:

> We came to the coastline of the Lotus Eaters,
> who live upon that flower. We landed there
> to take on water. All ship's companies
> mustered alongside for the mid-day meal.
> Then I sent out two picked men and a runner
> to learn what race of men that land sustained.
> They fell in, soon enough, with Lotus Eaters,
> who showed no will to do us harm, only
> offering the sweet Lotus to our friends –
> but those who ate this honeyed plant, the Lotus,
> never cared to report, nor to return:
> they longed to stay forever, browsing on
> that native bloom, forgetful of their homeland.
>
> (Homer 1998: 9.92–104)

Unlike the female monsters and enchantresses elsewhere, the Lotus Eaters mean no harm. Yet the magic plant works powerfully on Odysseus' men, so that he must force them wailing back to the ships. This episode reminds us of the considerable energy that the narrative exerts in order to remain a quest. Much like Odysseus' men, readers of romance must be summarily hauled from the pleasures of stasis and embarked on new episodes.

There are interesting echoes of Circe, who is first introduced weaving at her loom, in Odysseus' faithful wife. Penelope's most famous delaying tactic against the suitors is to promise that she will choose one of them when she has finished weaving a shroud for Odysseus' aged father, Laertes (Homer 1998: 2.103–14). But Penelope unweaves each night what she weaves during the day, and thus manages to hold off the suitors for three years before she is finally betrayed by her maids. Her weaving on the loom becomes a powerful metaphor for the narrative itself, as it advances and retreats with each obstacle to Odysseus' return. Yet even though her weaving associates her with both the dissembling and the delay that characterize enchantresses like Circe and other figures of female depravity, Penelope remains eminently virtuous. In her case, delay enables, rather than obstructs, the possibility of Odysseus' ultimate return.

For the cunning Penelope as for her husband, shape-shifting and tale-telling are survival strategies. Strikingly, these characterize the hero and heroine as much as their antagonists, virtually animating the narrative. While the *Odyssey* participates in the idealizing that is typical of romance, it does not idealize in simple moral terms. Odysseus is cunning, but not always a good leader: he often puts his men at risk unnecessarily, as in the Cyclops episode. He lies when necessary, and is ruthless in furthering his individual goals. In particular, the constant emphasis on disguised identity and surprising revelation suggests that transparency is not particularly valued. Instead, the wish-fulfillment of romance is intimately connected to the pleasure of delayed resolution and extended narrative.

Odysseus' disguises and lies provide the occasion for that much more storytelling. In fact, he invents even more adventures than he has actually experienced, and gives no less than five false accounts of himself, to everyone from Athena to Laertes. This multiplication of the plot into many false accounts provides an additional set of narrative detours. The trickery also offers the possibility of spectacular scenes of testing and recognition, as Odysseus' family and servants gradually realize who he is. These scenes essentially structure the second half of the poem, as Odysseus assembles the team of loyal companions that will enable him to vanquish the suitors (Murnaghan 1987: 20). While romance features transformations and deceit, it also enshrines the notion of an essential identity that can be revealed by signs. Thus Odysseus' aged nurse finds a scar from an old hunting wound; his hound recognizes his master's voice; Penelope herself confirms that he is her husband by testing his knowledge of their marvelous bed, hewn from a living tree around which the house is built.

In historical terms, the successful return of Odysseus, his defeat of the suitors, and his reunion with Penelope served as a powerful model of the *Nostos*, or returning hero. As Irad Malkin has observed, the figure of Odysseus was especially meaningful for the Greeks who, from the ninth century BC on, sailed beyond Ithaca to explore, trade, and colonize: "The resourceful, persevering, self-made man was the appropriate hero for people who sailed away *and* expected to return" (Malkin 1998: 2). Thus the Odyssean romance serves to animate early voyages from the safety of home to unknown geographies, essentially reversing Odysseus' own itinerary in the poem. The success of the hero's quest for home, however delayed, encourages countless quests for distant lands. Despite the often wandering energies of romance, that is, it may still serve the interest of far more deliberate enterprises.

THE GENRE OF "GREEK ROMANCE"

> The entire form of the Greek romance can be considered an elaboration of the period between initial desire and final consummation.
>
> John J. Winkler, "The Invention of Romance," 28

> In Greek romance . . . the normal means of transportation is by shipwreck.
>
> Northrop Frye, *The Secular Scripture*, 4

Whereas the *Odyssey* constantly complicates its protagonist, emphasizing the humanity and fallibility of the hero, the fictions traditionally known as Greek or, more precisely, Hellenistic romances are characterized by a strategy of idealization and wish-fulfillment. Yet they share with the *Odyssey* an emphasis on delay and postponement as the main engines of narrative interest, strategies that are, indeed, the very sources of the narrative. They are centrally concerned with *erōtika pathēmata*, or the sufferings of love. As a genre, this group of prose fictions features a similar boy-meets-girl plot in each case, characterized as follows by B.P. Reardon:

> A handsome youth and a beautiful girl meet by chance and fall in love, but unexpected obstacles obstruct their union; they are separated, and each is launched on a series of journeys and dangerous adventures; through all their tribulations, however, they remain faithful to each other and to the benevolent deities who at critical junctures guide their steps; and eventually they are reunited and live happily ever after.
>
> (Reardon 1991: 5)

From the vantage point of many centuries of romance this all seems trite, but John J. Winkler makes a convincing argument for the oddity of this plot in a society that actually regarded marriage as an institution fully separate from romantic love. In a seminal essay entitled "The Invention of Romance," Winkler suggests that the "love-leading-to-marriage" story – that is, the idea of conflating eros and marriage – may well have been imported to Greece from the Near East, first in the *Odyssey* itself and later in the idealizing romances (Winkler 1994: 36).

Part of the originality of these narratives lies in their focus on the experience of private individuals. If the *Odyssey* is remarkable for its relative effacement of corporate values as it emphasizes the heroic singularity and aloneness of Odysseus, these later fictions take individuation even further, as they relate the extraordinary adventures of ordinary mortals, albeit ones of high station, in a complex world. The setting is a crucial part of the story, with characters tossed about by both literal storms and the workings of inscrutable fate in a wide world of unfamiliar locales and exotic settings. Historically, these texts reflect the fractured and hybrid reality of the Hellenistic and early Roman periods, when the relative cultural homogeneity of Greek civilization gave way to the multiplicity of an imperial world. Greeks in the Near East were exposed to a variety of other cultures, while natives of these areas learned Greek. The fertile cultural cross-pollination of this world may well explain the late appearance of these complex narrative fictions. While the context was broadened and enriched, the individual's place within was proportionally reduced. Moreover, identity and experience in such a world were much less fixed, determined less by membership in a community than by chance, travel, or circumstance (Perry 1967: 48).

The characters in Greek romance suffer constantly the effects of greater forces. While they are hardly passive, they face repeated obstacles to any enterprise – fate seems to have it in for them no matter what they do. Neither are all the heroes of these stories men. In fact, the female protagonists are often markedly more active and resourceful than their male partners. And as they are constantly the object of unwanted attentions, they are called on to exercise that resourcefulness to protect both their chastity and their lives. In a sense, the single-minded fidelity of the characters functions as a kind of textual remedy to the indeterminacy of identity in a fundamentally dislocated world. The erotic attachment is the one thing that remains unchanging as hero and heroine move through a vast geography.

The five complete extant examples of what is conventionally known as Greek romance, in the narrow generic sense, with their probable dates, are Chariton's *Chaereas and Callirhoe* (first century AD), Xenophon of Ephesus' *Ephesiaca* (second century AD), Achilles Tatius' *Leucippe and Clitophon* (late second century AD), Longus' *Daphnis and Chloe* (late second century AD), and Heliodorus' *Ethiopica* (third or fourth century AD). Most of these datings are regarded as provisional. Given the intense new interest in these texts, it is likely that new evidence will force critics to reevaluate their dates. Their action is set several centuries before the date of composition, at the high point of Greek culture. The titles of the "big five" refer either to the pair of lovers or to a significant place in the development of the story (several are known by alternate titles, so that *Ethiopica*, for example, is also referred to as *Theagenes and Charicleia*), reflecting the importance not only of the central love story but of the extended imperial geography within these fictions.

Although these texts are less concerned with monsters than the *Odyssey*, their locales often provide a geographic rationale for marvels and magic. Critics have also suggested that many of their apparently fantastic details, as well as their structure, may derive from popular religious cults and the myths associated with them (Stephens and Winkler 1995: 314–15). Often, however, the narratives tax verisimilitude most heavily in their constant reliance on coincidence and chance. The *deus ex machina* of authorial dictum intervenes again and again both to shatter the characters' hopes and to rescue them from a certain death at the very last minute. It is exhausting even to read about these extreme reversals, but part of the generic "contract," so to speak, is that the perils and pitfalls will, however improbably, lead to a happy ending.

For our purposes here, I will take Heliodorus' *Ethiopica* as a paradigmatic case of the idealizing romance. It is generally considered the most sophisticated of the five central texts, and enjoyed a wide following among writers and critics in early modern Europe, including Cervantes and Racine, who, as the story goes, memorized the text after having it repeatedly confiscated and burned by his teachers (Winkler 1994: 23–4). Heliodorus makes constant reference to the *Odyssey*, underscoring the poem's important role as a romance precursor, while also developing his own highly elaborate structure and narrative stance. The story of the young lovers' meeting at a religious festival and of the much-deferred consummation of their love is also, simultaneously, a story of the return to origins, a narrative restoration of order and identity.

The opening of *Ethiopica* is widely admired as an example of both *in medias res* immediacy and almost cinematic perspectivism:

The smile of daybreak was just beginning to brighten the sky, the sunlight to catch the hilltops, when a group of men in brigand gear peered over the mountain that overlooks the place where the Nile flows into the sea at the mouth that men call the Heracleotic. They stood there for a moment, scanning the expanse of sea beneath them: first they gazed out over the ocean, but as there was nothing sailing there that held out hope of spoil and plunder, their eyes were drawn to the beach nearby. This is what they saw: a merchant ship was riding there, moored by her stern, empty of crew but laden with freight. This much could be surmised even from a distance, for the weight of her cargo forced the water up to the third line of boards on the ship's side. But the beach! – a mass of newly slain bodies, some of them quite dead, others half-alive and still twitching, testimony that the fighting had only just ended. To judge by the signs this had been no proper battle. Amongst the carnage were the miserable remnants of festivities that had come to this unhappy end. There were tables still set with food, and others upset on the ground, held in dead men's hands; in the fray they had served some as weapons, for this had been an impromptu conflict; beneath other tables men had crawled in the vain hope of hiding there. There were wine bowls upturned, and some slipping from the hands that held them; some had been drinking from them, others using them like stones, for the suddenness of the catastrophe had caused objects to be put to strange, new uses and taught men to use drinking vessels as missiles. There they lay, here a man felled by an axe, there another struck down by a stone picked up then and there from the shingly beach; here a man battered to death with a club, there another burned to death with a brand from the fire. Various were the forms of their deaths, but most were the victims of arrows and archery. In that small space the deity had contrived an infinitely varied spectacle, defiling wine with blood and unleashing war at the party, combining wining and dying, pouring of drink and spilling of blood, and staging this tragic show for the Egyptian bandits.

> They stood on the mountainside like the audience in a theater, unable
> to comprehend the scene . . .
>
> (Heliodorus 1989: 1.1)

Brigands, an abandoned ship, a mysterious and bloody battle: Heliodorus
sets the stage for romance adventures while postponing any explanation.
This combination of spectacular action and delayed exposition characterizes
the whole of the *Ethiopica*; the powerful effect of the narrative on its
readers depends on the conjunction of these two romance strategies.

Heliodorus seems quite conscious of the effect his text might have on
its readers. Note how the pirates' reaction when they first discover the
athletic Charicleia in her fine attire evokes the position of the reader:

> When she stood up, she seemed to them larger and more godlike, her
> weapons rattling at the sudden movement, the gold thread in her robe
> flashing in the sun, her hair tossing under her crown like a bacchante's
> and cascading over her back. They were terrified; but their incompre-
> hension of the scene caused them greater terror than the mere sight
> of it. Some said she must be a god – the goddess Artemis, or the
> Isis they worship in those parts; others said she was a priestess
> possessed by one of the gods and that she was responsible for the
> carnage before them. This is what they thought, but they did not yet
> know the truth.
>
> (Heliodorus 1989: 1.2)

"The truth" will not be known to the reader for some time, until Charicleia
herself explains how she and Theagenes came to the bloody beach. But by
the time she tells this story, the reader knows she is lying: she passes her
lover off as her brother in order not to alienate the robber chief who,
inevitably, wants to marry her (Heliodorus 1989: 1.21–2). How much of
her story, then, can we trust, especially when the narrator compares it to
a "siren spell" (Heliodorus 1989: 1.23)? Moreover, as we gradually realize,
Charicleia herself is unaware of her own origins. Unlike Odysseus, who
could at least choose to tell his real story, Charicleia cannot be relied on,
even when she is not attempting to disguise the facts.

Heliodorus further complicates the narrative exposition by constantly
reminding the reader of the tale's theatricality. The characters themselves

are highly self-conscious: Charicleia theatrically asks the pirates to "Kill us and so bring our story to a close" (Heliodorus 1989: 1.3). Cnemon, the Athenian who befriends the lovers, echoes Charicleia's dramatic language: his life, he tells us, is a subject for tragedy: "This is no time to introduce a new theme into your own tragedy in the form of my misfortunes" (Heliodorus 1989: 1.8). Several characters refer, too, to the improbability of events that seem motivated exclusively by a *deus ex machina*, the extraneous intervention that is the desperate recourse of writers and storytellers. Thus the reader is constantly reminded of the deliberate constructedness of romance narrative, with its emphasis on surprising effects and strategic revelations.

The movement of *Ethiopica* is twofold: even as the lovers Theagenes and Charicleia progress through a seemingly endless series of adventures such as capture, betrayal, repeated battles, and so forth, the narrative *regresses* to establish the origins of the mysterious heroine, which are not fully confirmed until the end of the text. In order to sustain the suspense, Heliodorus employs a complex narrative structure that multiplies the flashbacks of the *Odyssey*. Several characters provide partial accounts of Charicleia's history, their narrations framed within each other like Russian dolls.

Cnemon, whose role in the text is largely that of an audience for the protagonists' story and who has been separated from them as they escape the bandits, encounters the Egyptian prophet Calasiris. When importuned for his story, the old man sighs, "'It is an Odyssey of woe'" (Heliodorus 1989: 2.21). He so delays his narrative that Cnemon charges him with a slipperiness of obvious Homeric vintage: "So take your narrative back to what you promised. So far I have found you just like Proteus of Pharos, not that you take on false and shifting forms as he did, but you are forever trying to lead me in the wrong direction!" (Heliodorus 1989: 2.24).

Calasiris finally launches into the story of his travels from Egypt to Delphi, where he met Charicles, priest of Apollo and apparent father of Charicleia. In a neat chiasmus, the Greek priest himself had earlier traveled to Egypt to console himself after the death of his actual daughter. There, he tells Calasiris, he had met a black Ethiopian gymnosophist (a member of an ascetic Eastern sect) who entrusted him with the care of a beautiful young girl, a substitute daughter whom Charicles takes to Delphi and names Charicleia.

But the recursive story does not end there: embedded within Charicles' own narrative is the Ethiopian's account of how he had rescued the girl after she was exposed as a baby. Yet Charicles never finds out her actual origins – the Ethiopian fails to appear for a second meeting. Thus the reader is similarly left hanging, and it is not until Calasiris relates how, once in Delphi, he deciphered the Ethiopian royal script on the ribbon left with the abandoned Charicleia that we can piece together the story (Heliodorus 1989: 4.8). The ribbon encodes yet one more framed narrative, in this case that of Charicleia's mother, Persinna, Queen of the Ethiopians. The Queen explains that she has been forced to abandon the child because of her unusual skin color. Charicleia is born white because Persinna gazed on a painting of the naked Andromeda while she was conceived, and not through any act of adultery. Nonetheless, fearing an accusation of adultery for bearing her husband a white child, Persinna exposes the baby along with the ribbon and a magic ring, so that she can be both identified and protected from harm. Finally, the title by which we know the text makes sense!

Calasiris convinces Charicleia that Persinna has sent him to reclaim her daughter (although there is no independent confirmation of any sort for his claims), and that she must exchange "the life of an outcast in a foreign land" for restitution to "the throne that is yours" (Heliodorus 1989: 4.13). Thus the narrative echoes the *Odyssey*'s conjunction of quest and return, although of course Charicleia has no memory of her "home." From this point onwards, *Ethiopica* is as much the story of a search for origins as the story of the consummation of the love between Theagenes and Charicleia. Although the protagonists seldom have any say in their exact destination, and can barely be said to be searching for Ethiopia, Calasiris' exhortation prompts them to escape from Delphi and begin their adventures together. Charicleia's reunion with – and acceptance by – her parents in Ethiopia is as much part of the climax of the narrative as her eventual marriage to Theagenes.

Heliodorus mines the scene of recognition for all it's worth, endowing Charicleia with a black birthmark that both serves to identify her and complicates her whiteness, confronting her with the abandoned Charicles as well as with her birth-parents, and threatening the lovers with becoming sacrificial victims. The suspense builds and builds, until a resolution is achieved not only for the protagonists but for the society they rejoin: on the recommendation of the gymnosophist Sisimithres, the same wise Ethiopian who had rescued Charicleia and entrusted her to Charicles in Egypt, human sacrifice is abolished.

The conclusion suggests a particular concern with identity and community, and with what we would call race, but also with self-determination and the sanctity of the individual. Both indicate an active engagement with social mores, even within what has traditionally been labeled escapist fiction. As Margaret Doody has pointed out, narratives such as Heliodorus' sympathetically explore the position of those who were least powerful in Greek society: women and slaves. In fact, the very condition of slavery is interrogated, as noble characters are repeatedly subjected to violence and deprived of their freedom through the perverse workings of fate. Doody notes that this contradicts the Aristotelian notion of inferior beings naturally suited to slavery; in this world slavery is the result of violent force, and not natural at all. Thus the episodic adventures and trials of romance are not necessarily escapist; they challenge the truisms of the society that produced it (Doody 1996: 40–2). Doody's insight is an important corrective to readings of romance that emphasize its ultimate wish-fulfillment while disregarding the often complex picture of suffering and subjugation that precedes the resolution.

The emphasis on identity and community ultimately traced to a remote location suggests the extent to which Greek romance stretched and conflated the boundaries of the known world. In the case of *Ethiopica*, that world stretches from the omphalos of Delphi through a tumultuous Egypt to the far confines of Ethiopia, a land full of strange practices and monstrous creatures like the "camelopard" (recognizable to us as the giraffe; Heliodorus 1989: 10.27). But the connections between geography and identity in *Ethiopica* are strikingly tenuous. Charicleia, whom we are initially encouraged to regard as Greek, in contrast to the barbarian bandits, turns out to be radically foreign (Perkins 1999: 200–1). Despite her whiteness and her command of the Greek language, she is an Ethiopian, descended from the Sun, whom Persinna identifies as "the founder of our race" (Heliodorus 1989: 4.8). The final lines of the text suggest an author who, despite writing a Greek text, is similarly related to the sun and capable of moving across cultures: "So concludes the *Ethiopica*, the story of Theagenes and Charicleia, the work of a Phoenician from the city of Emesa, one of the clan of Descendants of the Sun, Theodosios's son, Heliodorus" (Heliodorus 1989: 10.41). As Stephens and Winkler point out, "It is not important that any of these statements be true, only that such a cultural hybrid was plausible to the ancient reader" (Stephens and Winkler 1995: 14).

Narratives such as *Ethiopica*, with their particular geographical breadth and investment in hybridity, may have emerged from the translation or adaptation of native stories into Greek during the early years of Rome's empire, when culture remained broadly Hellenistic despite Rome's ascendance, and Greek gradually became a *lingua franca* for culture as well as political administration (Stephens and Winkler 1995: 13–18). The interaction between Greeks and Hellenized non-Greeks, these critics argue, is the most obvious source for texts "all too often located in non-Greek lands, populated with non-Greek characters, and preoccupied with non-Greek cultures" (Stephens and Winkler 1995: 17–18). Two of the central romance strategies of the *Ethiopica* – the episodic string of adventures and the delayed exposition – may well reflect the demands placed on a narrative that attempted to encompass a broader, more complex world, in which persons were subject to sudden and often unmotivated changes of status and, indeed, identity across a wider geographic expanse.

While the texts of Chariton, Xenophon and Achilles Tatius are similar to Heliodorus' in their geographic reach, Longus' *Daphnis and Chloe* presents some marked differences. This text is above all a pastoral, a rural idyll rather than a narrative of travel and exotic adventures. It is set entirely in Greece, more precisely in the town of Mytilene on the island of Lesbos, with a minor excursion to the neighboring Methymnaea. This is a much narrower and more manageable world. Even when pirates appear, they too are Greeks, from Pyrrha, although they use a Carian ship in order to pass themselves off as foreigners. The primary axis of difference, as befits a pastoral, is between country and city dwellers. The two protagonists, who are exposed as children, nursed by animals, and rescued by simple rural folk, herd their flocks together and tentatively explore the mysteries of love.

Yet for all its generic differences *Daphnis and Chloe* illustrates the way in which romance, as a literary strategy, may inhabit different genres and forms. The central strategies of Longus' text: the delay of sexual consummation as the would-be lovers gradually achieve knowledge of the world and of themselves, the idealization of the protagonists despite their apparently humble status, the revelation of their exalted origins and their restoration, are hardly specific to the pastoral. In fact, they resonate both with *Ethiopica* and with a set of texts that far exceeds that category.

Here is where the notion of romance as strategy becomes especially useful. It allows us to recognize that Longus' text is set in a pastoral world, and is thus radically different from the other texts with which it is indiscriminately grouped in the hodgepodge category of "Greek romance." Yet at the same time it highlights the commonplaces and narrative maneuvers that the texts share, regardless of generic affiliation. The notion of romance strategy becomes especially useful as we recognize the bewildering variety of texts that have been described as classical romances. There is more to be gained by identifying the similarities and continuities among these texts, I suggest, than by stressing their differences. The most responsible way to do this is often to suspend the category of genre as organizing principle, and replace it with a smaller-scale set of elements, identifiable as *romance strategies* within texts that might belong to any number of genres. This approach also bypasses the controversy over what some critics charge are the implicit limits of romance as genre, a controversy that I will survey below.

Focusing on romance strategies instead of on a closed romance genre can also challenge the unexamined insularity of generic categories. Thus we can recover the place of texts like *Apollonius of Tyre*, which presents important similarities to the "big five," but could never be classified as "Greek romance" because only a later Latin version (tentatively dated to the fifth or sixth century AD), hypothetically identified as a reworking of an earlier Greek text, remains. Critics are not entirely sure how to characterize *Apollonius*, primarily because they have largely categorized romance as a Greek form. David Konstan, for example, who emphasizes its differences, argues that Apollonius should be considered a "distinctly Latin narrative" (Konstan 1994: 181), but the text in fact shares several crucial strategies with the "Greek romance."

The plot of *Apollonius*, which is the principal source for Shakespeare's *Pericles*, is as eventful as that of *Ethiopica*, with separations and shipwrecks that strew the characters throughout the eastern Mediterranean. The primary difference is that the privileged relationships within the text are not between lovers, but between fathers and daughters (Konstan 1994: 178–80). The text begins with a violent preamble: King Antiochus of

Antioch first rapes his only daughter, who is brought to the verge of suicide by the incest, and subsequently challenges her suitors with impossible riddles. Yet when Apollonius, Prince of Tyre, solves the riddle by recognizing the incest, Antiochus attempts to have him murdered instead of giving up his daughter. Apollonius is forced to flee his kingdom in order to save his life. After this sobering introduction, the adventures of Apollonius begin in earnest. He is shipwrecked and helped by a fisherman, eventually coming to the attention of the king of Cyrene. The king's daughter studies with him and promptly falls in love. Although her father agrees to the marriage and they are happily united, she apparently dies in childbirth while on a voyage to claim Antiochus' throne. Her coffin is set adrift and lands at Ephesus, where she is revived and becomes a priestess of Diana. The distraught Apollonius leaves his young daughter, whom he names Tarsia, with friends in Tarsus while he travels to Egypt as a merchant.

But the beautiful Tarsia is too much of a threat for the friends' own daughter. The wife arranges to have her murdered. In the nick of time, she is captured instead by pirates, but not before her aged nurse reveals her true origins to her. The pirates sell her to a brothel-owner in Mytilene, but Tarsia manages to preserve her virginity by entertaining people with music and riddles. When he returns to Tarsus for her and learns of her supposed death, Apollonius sails off in desperation. A storm brings him to Mitylene, and Tarsia is sent on board his ship to cheer him. Although the scene echoes the incest-plot of the introduction, Apollonius makes no advances to the young woman. He eventually recognizes her as his daughter; she marries the nobleman who had protected her in the brothel, and all prepare to return to Tarsus. But a vision orders Apollonius to go to Ephesus instead and relate his story in the temple of Diana. His wife promptly recognizes him, completing the family reunion. Apollonius distributes punishments and rewards, and all regain their rightful position.

Obviously, separation and restitution, chastity and constancy are all as important in *Apollonius* as in the texts traditionally classified as Greek romances. The narrative delay and the repeated misfortunes echo what we have seen in both the *Odyssey* and *Ethiopica*, although the narration itself is more straightforward. The links between the episodes are less deliberate than in either of those texts; Northrop Frye considers *Apollonius* a good example of an "and then" narrative, where new episodes are relatively unmotivated, as opposed to the more sophisticated "hence" narrative that describes a causal relationship among events (Frye 1976: 47–9). Yet there is a certain degree of symbolic repetition, underscoring the circularity of the restitution plot: repeated encounters between Apollonius and a young woman; repeated recourse to storms that disrupt the characters' plans and riddles that serve to test them or bring them together (Archibald 1991: 12–13). There are also explicit references to what we can already identify as a romance tradition: Apollonius' warm reception by the princess evokes the Nausicaa episode of the *Odyssey*, and her pining for the hero is rendered through actual quotations from Dido's passion for Aeneas in Book IV of the *Aeneid* (Konstan 1994: 176–7).

For our purposes, what is most striking is the central narrative of a quest that the characters only barely understand, and which in some cases is completely opaque to them. Presumably they would all wish for the reconstitution of their family (although it is never clear why Apollonius' wife never searches for him or their daughter), yet they rarely have enough information to seek that goal directly. Instead, they are reduced to aimless wandering, and it is only through the operation of a fairly heavy-handed *deus ex machina*, in the form of storms, pirates, dream visions and amazing coincidences, that they can be reunited and their true identities revealed. The characters' agency is significantly reduced, as the narrative patterns of romance take over. Verisimilitude or realism is emphatically not the point.

ROMANCE OR NOVEL? SOME RECENT CONTROVERSIES, AND A LARGER MAP OF ROMANCE

In recent years, some critics have decisively rejected the term "romance" to refer to the prose narratives of antiquity. Margaret Doody, whose work I first discussed in the Introduction, has been one of the most vocal proponents of adopting the term "novel" for all longer prose fiction. Doody suggests that the dyad romance/novel always implies a distinction in quality: "romance" is primitive, static, unsophisticated, while "novel" is evolved, articulate, complex. Moreover, she points out, in this distinction there is always an implicit teleology at work: the romance will become the novel once it finally grows up (Doody 1996: 1–5 and passim). In order to do away with this teleological understanding, in which prose fiction finally comes of age with the English eighteenth-century novel, Doody proposes to do without the term romance altogether, and to use "novel" for all prose fiction of a certain length (Doody 1996: 16). Only the change in terminology, Doody suggests, will force critics to acknowledge and appreciate the full complexity of the longer Hellenistic fictions, traditionally known – and derided – as romances.

Doody clearly hopes that the change in terminology will dislodge the influential opinion of critics like the Russian formalist Mikhail Bakhtin, who have emphasized the relative simplicity of the "ancient novel," as Doody calls it. Bakhtin argues that all change in these texts occurs across space, with no permanent change through time. Their "chronotope," as Bakhtin terms the way in which the texts represent time and space, may be bracketed off as an interlude; the protagonists never change or develop as a result of their adventures (Bakhtin 1981: 89–90). As David Konstan usefully points out, implicit in Bakhtin's assessment of these prose narratives is the expectation, based on modern romantic fiction, that the love relationship will change over the course of the text, along an axis of moral development (Konstan 1994: 45–6). Bakhtin even specifies what the preferable alternative would consist of:

> If the situation were otherwise – had, for example, the initial instantaneous passion of the heroes grown stronger as a result of their adventures and ordeals; had that passion been tested in action, thereby acquiring new qualities of a stable and tried love; had the heroes themselves matured, come to know each other better – then we would have an example of a much later European novel-type, one that would not be an adventure novel at all, and certainly not a Greek romance.
>
> (Bakhtin 1981: 90)

The "ancient novel"'s failure to conform to this expectation signals for Bakhtin its primitiveness and inadequacy, and hence, we gather, its designation as romance. This judgment ignores the many ways, such as narrative patterning and structure, point of view, symbolism, in which texts like *Ethiopica* are undeniably complex, even if character development is not their strong suit. Moreover, as I have suggested earlier, it may be that the fixity of the erotic object, and the characters' unwavering, unchanging desire in a disordered world is precisely the point.

Yet critics such as Doody and Konstan implicitly accept the hierarchical distinction between romance and novel; they simply want to replace the former term with the latter when discussing texts that they appreciate. My project here is to eschew the often unspoken distinctions of value or sophistication and focus instead on how these texts work, on what connects them to each other and to a particular literary genealogy. "Romance," I will argue, is a much more precise term for those connections and that genealogy than "novel" could ever be. More importantly, it does not matter whether we classify the texts as "Greek romances" or "ancient novels"; what matters for our purposes is identifying the relevant mechanisms and topoi within them.

The problems of classification are particularly fraught within the field of classics, because the corpus changes in unexpected ways. Since the "romances" were first characterized as such, the emergence of new papyri containing fragments of prose fiction has posed an ongoing challenge to the older generic classification. The five texts conventionally regarded as the core of the "Greek romance" genre may not, it turns out, reflect its full extent or variability: "Fragmentary novels may well reveal, however, that the so-called ideal romantic is no more than a subclass of the whole, whose survival says more about the tastes of subsequent late antique and Byzantine readers than it does about the field of ancient novels itself" (Stephens and Winkler 1995: 5). Some of these fragments, like *Ninus*, the story of the Assyrian prince Ninus and his consort Semiramis, have been known since the late nineteenth century; others were first published as recently as the 1970s, and their study is just beginning.

Stephens and Winkler's speculations about the fragmentary corpus of the "ancient novel" suggest the advantage of retaining a sense of romance as strategy. This approach allows us to recognize romance within a variety of genres, and to separate the definition of romance from the problems of taxonomy. As these critics point out, interpenetrability and idiosyncrasy characterize classical prose fiction: "The pool of ancient narrative types seems to have been at once fluid and flexible, the absorption of other literary types more a matter of individual experiment than of generic determinatives" (Stephens and Winkler 1995: 9). In this context, taxonomic exertions seem unadvisable.

Even without the evidence of the new discoveries, however, the occurrence of romance in classical texts can hardly be limited to the handful of

"Greek romances" traditionally identified as the entire genre. If, as I have suggested here, we focus on romance strategies, it becomes possible to map romance across a wide range of texts, from an epic poem like the *Odyssey* to several kinds of texts that were not even presented to their readers as fictions per se. These include everything from imaginative biographies of famous personages (*The Life and Acts of Alexander of Macedon*, commonly known as *The Alexander Romance*), in which marvels, presages, and restitution figure in important ways, to descriptions of marvelous travels in unknown lands (the *Wonders beyond Thule* of Antonius Diogenes, now known only from a later summary), to biographical gospels or "acts" (the *Pseudo-Clementine Recognitions* or the *Acts of Thomas*) and hagiography – the narratives of saints' lives – in which erotic sufferings are transmuted into "Christian and para-Christian narratives of adventure" (Reardon 1991: 165–8).

These texts, and the ones discussed above, illustrate the ubiquity and malleability of romance as a set of strategies that organize and animate narrative. These strategies consist of the complication or delay of a linear quest; first, by the successive deployment of obstacles to progress, where eros can function either as an impediment to the quest or as its very goal, and, second, by the circularity of the narrative, expressed both in the importance of revelations, returns, and restorations and in the doubling or flashbacks of the narratives themselves. In this sense, romance seems like the bedrock of narrative if not one of its most important strata, although not in the archetypal sense that Northrop Frye might propose, but in a narratological one. Yet, as subsequent chapters will repeatedly show, romance involves not only strategies of form, but the privileging of a certain content, already evident in its classical manifestations: occluded and subsequently revealed identities, idealized protagonists, marvels and monsters, tasks and tests. The striking repetition of these elements in medieval romance suggests that, regardless of its critical reception then and now, classical romance had a long and influential afterlife.

2

MEDIEVAL ROMANCE

And with that word he drew towards the fire
And took a light, and framed his countenance
As if to gaze upon an old romance.
Chaucer, Troilus and Criseyde

Although medieval romance is the corpus most readily identified as a genre
by present-day critics, the term originally referred not to a class of texts
but to a linguistic and literary operation: the transformation of Latin texts
into French. "Romance" derives from the Old French expression "mettre
en romanz" – to translate into the vernacular, or romance, language.
Generic boundaries for these texts were originally very fluid: many kinds
of narratives in the vernacular were called romances, but also "estoires"
(stories/histories) or "contes" (tales) (Krueger 2000: 1). The construction
of a recognizable genre out of this varied and enormous literature has
required considerable critical energy; it is as though, in our day, critics
attempted to designate the Loeb Classical Library – the Harvard University
Press series of Greek and Latin texts in dual-language editions – as a genre.
But the attempt at classification has been helped along by occasional highly
self-conscious references to romance within the texts themselves, as in the

epigraph above, and by the strong intertextuality in a corpus of stories that reappears from one text to the next, from one author to another, and across several vernaculars. In this sense, "Any given romance appears simultaneously as a whole or a fragment with respect to that larger intertextual dialogue" (Bruckner 2000: 14). The iterability of romance is a key sign of its cultural currency and historical importance. The romance that repeats "descends to us as the aggregated work of many minds, many hands, and many efforts over the centuries: as the material concretion of the collective will of cultural agents and forces acting over time to preserve, develop, and transmit a story felt to be important" (Heng 2003: 8).

Interestingly, in the field of medieval studies, unlike in Classics, romance is not considered a term of opprobium. More accessible than hagiography (accounts of the lives of saints) or the *chansons de geste* (epic poems on heroic deeds), romance appeals to modern readers and has been granted a privileged place by critics, relative to its actual role in medieval literary culture (Gaunt 2000: 48). Due to this critical predilection, romance is the bread-and-butter of medieval literary studies, and both the primary and secondary bibliographies are enormous. In this field, romance patently avoids the critical scorn that marks it in other periods of literary history. Yet its very popularity can backfire: critics have pointed out the problematic metonymic association of romance with the Middle Ages, whereby the entire historical period is bathed in a sentimental glow of fanciful idealization. As Rita Copeland incisively notes, already by the sixteenth century "the definitive characteristic of romance is no longer its form, with which its very modernity was bound up, but its content: love, chivalry, adventure, the Arthurian 'golden age,' the exoticism and fancy of a distantly imagined past, indeed, everything associated with the word *aventure*" (Copeland 1991: 220).

This chapter provides an introduction to the medieval romance genre as it has been codified by critics, examining both the congruences and incongruences of the category. I then suggest how understanding romance as a strategy might yield a different corpus, cutting across traditional generic categories to encompass hagiography, *lais* and other vernacular forms.

COURTS, KNIGHTS, AND CLERKS

The genre of medieval romance is conventionally defined as the group of narratives in the vernacular that emerge around 1150 in the court of Henry II and Eleanor of Aquitaine in England (where Anglo-Norman, a form of French, was the elite language) and tell stories of love and adventure. Although generally situated in a distant classical or Arthurian past, the stories feature all the trappings of contemporary court and chivalric culture, so that, for example, Greek and Roman "knights" skirmish in patently medieval tournaments. The primary sources for this literature are Greek and Roman legends (the story of Thebes, the Trojan war) as well as specific classical texts (Virgil, Statius, Ovid's *Metamorphoses*, Apollonius), medieval historiography, Celtic legends, and the *chansons de geste*. Since the thirteenth century, romance has traditionally been divided into three subjects (although many texts classified as romances elude this early characterization): the matter of Rome, which includes primarily reworkings of the story of Troy and the *Aeneid*; the matter of Britain, which comprises the stories of King Arthur and his Knights of the Round Table; and the matter of France: stories of the French knights made famous by the *chansons de geste*. Although the characters might often resemble those of the earlier French epics, in romances there is a much greater emphasis on the private over the public, on the perspective of women, and on the knights' experience of love. While romance emerges in an Anglo-Norman context, it soon travels far beyond it, with the important German romance tradition, for example, imitating and elaborating on French sources.

Medieval romance emerges as an elite court genre, although the use of the vernacular allows it to reach a much wider audience than its origins would suggest. Generally, romances were initially recited to musical accompaniment before the assembled feudal household, and only some of them were recorded. The characters of romance are those same members of the secular court: kings and queens, knights and ladies, and retainers of various kinds. But the court is more than a setting: it often anchors the narrative with an almost centripetal force. The hero sets out from the court and returns to it once he has proven himself. Simon Gaunt explains this centrality in terms of the court's historical importance: "The court – a legal, financial, and social center – was the forum in which temporal power was exercised and established through rituals designed to demonstrate the lord's superiority. An intensely political environment, the court was also a place where individuals from a variety of cultural and social backgrounds met" (Gaunt 2000: 47). Romance thus takes its place among the cultural forms that celebrate the court and, as a cultural crossroad, the court becomes the setting for improbable encounters.

The courtly setting accounts for the frequent idealizing tone of medieval romance: in these stories (with some notable exceptions), all the ladies are beautiful, all the knights are valiant, even though the actual events of the plot often undercut the idealizing rhetoric. More importantly, idealization is often countered by a sharp reflection on society: given the political centrality of the court, romance reflects ideological conflicts, and addresses the precise historical context out of which it emerges. Although romance is frequently described as an escapist genre that erases or whitewashes social conflict, it presents a dialectical relation to court ideology. It is often skeptical of absolute distinctions between good and evil, civilized and uncivilized violence, and of the compatibility between erotic and military pursuits. Simply because the romance often deals with individual protagonists and their quests does not mean that it is not acutely concerned with their status as cultural fantasies. For example, the heroic identity that the protagonist achieves often leads to an actual position at court, thereby reinforcing the feudal system (Segre 1985: 19), yet the foibles of the hero or his antagonists often reflect badly on the court itself.

This double valence is built into the narrative structure of romance, as the narrator pointedly fails to identify with the lords and ladies of the story. Instead, he speaks for a class of authors who were most often clerks: men in the lower orders of the Church, who did not serve the role of modern clergy but instead performed administrative tasks for the court. Their essential attribute was their education, which included primarily the ability to read (and thus imitate) Latin texts. Their scholarly values of *clergerie* (clerkliness) differ markedly from the aristocratic, heroic *chevalerie* (chivalry) of romance heroes. Knights, that is, did not write romances. As critics have frequently noted, this distance between the clerkly narrator and the chivalric protagonists results in a pronounced irony in many romances, complicating the genre's ideological investments.

One fine example of the authorial irony that destabilizes the idealizing force of romance occurs in Chrétien de Troyes' *Erec and Enide* (c. 1170) As we will see, Chrétien was one of the most self-conscious of clerkly narrators. His account of an argument between King Arthur and one of his knights at the beginning of his tale, immediately after a glowing description of the court, is highly ironic. The king proposes that the court hunt for the famed white stag of ancient tradition, only to be contradicted immediately by Sir Gawain:

> My lord Gawain was not a bit pleased when he heard this. "Sire," said he, "from this hunt you will gain neither gratitude nor thanks. We have all known for a long time what tradition is attached to the white stag: he who can kill the white stag by right must kiss the most beautiful of the maidens of your court, whatever may happen. Great evil can come from this, for there are easily five hundred damsels of high lineage here, noble and wise daughters of kings; and there is not a one who is not the favourite of some valiant and bold knight, each of whom would want to contend, rightly or wrongly, that the one who pleases him is the most beautiful and the most noble."
>
> (Chrétien 1991: 37–8)

Gawain's warning about the dangers of both tradition and competition plays against the reader's expectations, especially since, given the court setting and the gathering of so many knights, we are prepared to admire ritual and combat. In part, Gawain's intervention questions romance's nostalgia for the past against which the contemporary court is measured, and hints at the individual flaws that will endanger chivalric culture in the future. But the knight reminds us also that the very narrative depends on the shattering of equilibrium at the court. Arthur's proposals will surely lead to conflict, but without that conflict there is no story to tell. The irony is compounded by Arthur's obdurate insistence on his royal prerogative: "This I know well, but I will not give up my plan for all that, for the word of a king must not be contravened" (Chrétien 1991: 38).

Ultimately, Arthur himself finds the stag and his choice of maiden is unanimously approved. Yet by pointing out the difficulty of resolving the beauty contest, Gawain challenges the idealizing conventions that Chrétien is establishing: if all damsels are equally beautiful, how is the court to choose among them? The answer – in other narratives if not in this one – is a dangerous perspectivism that threatens the unity of the court. Yet this perspectivism, which appears both ominous and paradoxically productive at the level of plot, is also a central narrative technique for Chrétien. What makes his stories so powerful is the interweaving of multiple perspectives, and the constant reminders that reality is apprehended very differently according to one's social position or allegiances.

Episodes such as Gawain's objection to Arthur's suggestion script the tension between the chivalric code and the clerkly narrator's often ironic perspective on it. The clerkly point of view may also be expressed more directly, in frequent asides that afford the narrator a considerable presence within the text. In the case of the more sophisticated narrators, like Chrétien, the reader is constantly reminded that there is a playful intelligence behind the narrative. Sometimes the narrator even refers obliquely to the material conditions of writing for a patron in the court, as in the slightly embarrassing praise of aristocratic generosity in Chrétien's *Cligés*: "Largesse alone makes one a worthy man, not high birth, courtesy, wisdom, gentility, riches" (Chrétien 1991: 125).

The narrative tension between *clergerie* and *chevalerie* is echoed at the level of content by the hero's own struggle to reconcile competing demands. As Cesare Segre points out, "The great invention of the medieval romancers was to link love to glorious deeds so as to make love the direct cause and heroic personal identity and social position the indirect consequences" (Segre 1985: 35). The uneasy conjunction of love and adventure is the motor for the narrative in countless romances, as heroes attempt to reconcile their often incompatible obligations to eros and to chivalry. Thus the basic quest through which the hero is initiated or proven in chivalric society is complicated by the parallel pressures of love. Yet, as Segre points out, the tension between eros and chivalry also "enables serial adventures to attain a meaningful unity in the face of the threatening centrifugal force of the fantastic," a unity reinforced by the fixed points of the hero's departure and return (Segre 1985: 36).

LOVE IN THE TIME OF CHIVALRY

While the tension between eros and adventure is a central romance motif that transcends the specifics of the medieval genre (think of Odysseus derailed on his voyage home, or of Aeneas lingering with Dido), in this period it reflects a series of important cultural transformations in the understanding of love and its relationship to chivalry. While modern critics still sometimes refer to this phenomenon as "courtly love," the term was never used by medieval authors, a discrepancy that complicates our attempts to reconstruct this set of beliefs and practices as a coherent ideology. Instead, as Sarah Kay usefully argues, we might think of "courtly love" as the representation of the many contradictions in erotic theory and practice in the period: "Courtly texts do not so much propound precepts as raise alternatives, permitting contradictions to surface, but within a restricted agenda of shared preoccupations. Is love foolish or moderate? Ecstatic or rational? Socially beneficial or anti-social? Spiritual or sensual?" (Kay 2000: 85)

The twelfth-century courtly context that saw the emergence of romance was characterized by a fascination with the Ovidian erotic tradition, particularly its sophisticated conception of love as a textual performance and its imagery of erotic oxymoron: love as suffering, painful pleasure, and so forth. The Ovidian heritage had been explored and developed in vernacular poetry some decades before the first romances, in the Provençal poetry of the troubadours in the circle of William, ninth Duke of Aquitaine, the same courtly context in which romance would emerge. Eleanor of Aquitaine, granddaughter of William and wife first of Louis VII of France, then Henry II of England, was an important patron of troubadours in her own right and instrumental in disseminating their tradition throughout her various courts. Her daughter Marie de Champagne, Chrétien's patron, encouraged her chaplain Andreas Capellanus to write a treatise on love, *The Art of Love* (c. 1180), which became hugely influential. Actual social practices at court such as the "love questions" or "courts of love" quickly became assimilated as literary conventions. These traditions provided a language for thinking about the relation between love and subjectivity, the tension between private feeling and public obligation, and the connection between eroticism and spirituality. Rather than a firm set of conventions, then, the notion of courtly love describes primarily an ongoing social negotiation over the place and import of love. Some of the earliest tales in the vernacular, as well as the most influential (*Piramus et Tisbé*, *Floire et Blancheflor*, the Tristan romances, the *Roman d'Eneas* discussed below), focus on erotic love and the challenges it faces. Chrétien's more sophisticated productions, such as *Cligés*, include detailed arguments about the signs, effects, and pitfalls of love, often presented as a character's internal monologue (Segre 1985: 29). Fenice, the heroine of *Cligés*, debates with herself whether the hero loves her:

> She was both prosecution and defence, arguing with herself as follows: "With what intent did Cligés say to me 'I am wholly devoted to you', if he was not prompted by Love? What rights do I have over him? Why should he prize me so much as to make me his sovereign lady? Is he not much fairer than I and of much higher rank? I can see nothing but love that could have granted me such a gift. Taking myself – who am incapable of escaping Love's power – as an example, I will prove that he would never have declared himself 'wholly mine' had he not loved me . . ."
>
> (Chrétien 1991: 176)

This kind of debate, which goes on at great length, locates the text within the courtly tradition of love casuistry while also enabling a more sustained development of characters' interiority.

Insofar as courtly love has a defined content, it involves the idealization of the lady, often already married to someone other than her lover, and the consequent valorization of either adultery or self-denial. Courtly love thus sits uneasily with religious strictures against adultery in the period, even as it couches erotic love in a language of idealization, mysticism, and Christian suffering. Its version of love as sacred pursuit is inherently sacrilegious. But the contradictions don't end there: while love propels the lover to great feats of heroism, it may also divert him from the pursuit of arms. (In general, and unlike the Greek romances discussed earlier, medieval romance is more interested in the masculine perspective on eros, although many describe the feminine viewpoint as well.) And although love contributes to the knight's personal or private virtue in the lay registers of refinement and courtesy, it also gets in the way of his public commitments.

The classic case of this particular paradox is the knight Lancelot, whose adultery with Queen Guinevere not only violates religious strictures in general, but also his specific feudal allegiance to King Arthur. In Chrétien's *The Knight of the Cart*, the earliest surviving narrative about the adulterous liaison, Lancelot's transgression is pointedly rendered in the language of religious devotion and suffering. Lancelot's love for Guinevere verges on idolatry: when he finds her comb, "he began to adore the hair. . . . He placed so much faith in these strands of hair that he felt no need for any other aid" (Chrétien 1991: 225). In order to save Guinivere, he must undergo repeated humiliations and sufferings, from riding the base cart of the title to crossing a bridge made out of a sharp sword, on which he cuts his hands, knees, and feet. As critics often point out, Lancelot appears in the story as a savior, even a redeemer, and his wounds are reminiscent of Christ's wounds on the Cross (Kay 2000: 81–2). Lancelot's night of love with Guinevere merits even more elaborate metaphors of religion: he bows to her and adores her, "for in no holy relic did he place such faith" (264), while leaving her constitutes "a true martyrdom, and he suffered a martyr's agony" (265). Such intense devotion to Lancelot's lord's wife is problematic both for its patently sacrilegious imitation of proper religious devotion and for its transgression against the feudal ties that bind Lancelot to Arthur. The story evinces the contradictions of courtly love and also its rigors: despite the huge cost of the affair to Lancelot and his self-abasement, even he cannot reach the ideal of the lover, because of his initial hesitation to do all that love demands.

In the story of Tristan and his beloved Iseult, developed from Celtic legend by multiple medieval poets, the betrayal of familial bonds compounds the breach of feudal ties: Tristan brings the beautiful princess from Ireland to Cornwall to marry his uncle, King Mark. So profoundly transgressive is the affair that Tristan must be relieved from his agency in the matter: his undying love for Iseult comes, we are told, from the inadvertent drinking of a magic potion. In the version in Thomas Malory's *Morte d'Arthur* (1469–70), where Sir Tristram of Lyoness is a knight of the Round Table and, significantly, second only to Lancelot, the transgression is defused by transforming King Mark into a despicable enemy.

Although the focus is most often on the knight's difficult choice between eros and other allegiances, the lady is not always a passive object of desire. One striking case of female agency is the popular thirteenth-century French romance *Aucassin and Nicolette* in which the heroine, who is a captive Saracen princess persecuted by her beloved's father, repeatedly takes her fate into her own hands, escaping from her tower prison, alerting the ineffectual Aucassin to her whereabouts, and finally cross-dressing as a minstrel in order to rejoin him. Yet, beyond its amazing depiction of a Saracen–Christian union, this text is unusual in that it does not problematize Aucassin's firm commitment to his beloved over his filial allegiance, as is more common. Another highly unusual case is the chivalric *Roman de Silence*, by Heldris de Cornuälle (late thirteenth century), which bears a curious relation to the Arthurian material. The protagonist, Silence, is a girl brought up as a boy in order to defy inheritance laws, who, while dressed as a man, becomes the object of the adulterous queen's desire. Yet her behavior is masculine throughout: she is knighted and distinguishes herself on the battlefield, saving her lord from his enemies. It is not until the very end of the narrative that she resumes her female identity, which has been revealed by her ability to capture Merlin, who could only be caught by a woman's trick.

Female agency also figures prominently in the English Arthurian poem *Sir Gawain and the Green Knight* (c. 1375). Although the contest at the center of the text is ostensibly Gawain's confrontation with a terrifying green stranger, the more important test comes from the Green Knight's lady, who repeatedly attempts to seduce the knight while her husband hunts in the forest. Her wooing mimics the appeals and offers more routinely associated with a knight trying to win a lady. As Geraldine Heng points out:

> Where it is usually the knight who comes into his identity as an active, desiring subject, a male courtly lover, through such commonplaces – by establishing a love relation with a desired female, the object of love, in time-honored custom – here it is the Lady who usurps the active masculine function, thereby unsettling with her activity the routine accomplishment of an orderly and familiar sexual identity by the courtly subject.
>
> (Heng 1992: 118–19)

Although the lady does not ultimately achieve the seduction, her power over Gawain is symbolized in her green girdle, which he accepts as a magical talisman to protect him but that becomes instead a sign of his weakness.

Romance thus incorporates the contradictions and complications of courtly love in several interesting ways. First, it reflects the enhanced role of eros in the culture, and the way that love takes over, however uncomfortably, the discourses of war and religion. Second, it incorporates the self-denial of courtly love into its own narrative structure: the erotic delay identified earlier as a romance strategy is newly animated by a contemporary belief in the value of erotic postponement. Most importantly, romance stages over and over again the tension between the pursuit of love and the pursuit of arms, presenting the lover as essentially compromised by the erotic drive that takes him away from his obligations. For the love of Guinevere, Lancelot is willing to betray not only his king but also his own self-image, as when he rides the lowly cart or abides by Guinevere's command that he "do his worst" in a tournament (Chrétien 1991: 276–7).

A wonderful example of this dynamic occurs, once again, in Chrétien's *Erec and Enide*, in which Erec stubbornly tackles an adventure ironically named "the Joy of the Court," but described by the king as "a most sorrowful subject" (Chrétien 1991: 106). In a beautiful garden of plenty, ringed by magic, Erec finds a set of stakes topped with the heads of knights, and one stake ominously uncapped. He turns to his beloved Enide to reassure her, emphasizing that love inspires him to take on dangerous adventures:

> I assure you that if the only bravery in me was that inspired by your love, yet I would not fear to do battle, hand to hand, with any man alive. I act foolishly, boasting like this, yet I do not say this out of pride, but only because I wish to comfort you.
>
> (Chrétien 1991: 109)

Erec proceeds alone, and finds a beautiful lady lying on a silver bed. Suddenly, a gigantic knight intrudes on the scene and challenges Erec to fight with him. After a long and arduous battle Erec defeats him, and agrees to reveal his name in return for the true story of the garden and the Joy. The defeated knight complies:

> Now hear who has kept me so long in this garden: as you have ordered, I wish to tell everything however much it may pain me. That maiden, who is sitting there, loved me from childhood and I loved her. It was a source of pleasure to us both and our love grew and improved until she asked a boon of me without first saying what it was. Who would refuse his lady anything? He is no lover who does not unhesitatingly do whatever pleases his lady, unstintingly and neglecting nothing, if ever he can in any way. . . . I made her a promise, but I did not know what

until after I became a knight. King Evrain, whose nephew I am, dubbed me in the sight of many gentlemen within this garden where we are. My lady, who is sitting there, immediately invoked my oath and said that I had sworn to her never to leave this place until some knight came along who defeated me in combat. It was right for me to remain rather than break my oath, though I wish I had never sworn it. Since I knew the good in her – in the thing that I held most dear – I could not show any sign that anything displeased me, for if she had noticed it she would have withdrawn her love and I did not wish that at any price, no matter what the consequences.

(Chrétien 1991: 111)

The knight in the garden had faced an exquisite predicament. (The verbal tense matters here – the story is only told once the bind has been dissolved, however shamefully.) Initially caught in the snare of the "rash boon" – a favorite romance motif – as he hastily promises to grant some as yet unknown favor to his lady, the knight is then firmly bound by the terms of the boon itself. Essentially, his lady manages to undo chivalry by placing it at the service of eros, an extreme case of the more subtle conflict that animates so many romances, including the primary story of Erec and Enide. The knight is prevented from either embarking on adventures, aiding his lord, or generally pursuing honor by the all-consuming vow of stasis that he must honor first. The only knights he may fight are those that come to him in his garden. And because the outer limit on his stasis, the prison of eros, is his *defeat* at arms, he must first suffer dishonor if he is to be liberated to pursue honor at all. As he explains to Erec, "I should have committed a grievous fault in holding back and not defeating all those I could overpower: such a deliverance would have been ignoble" (Chrétien 1991: 112). The episode neatly encapsulates the tension between love and chivalric adventure in romance, and while it places the blame for the stasis wholly on the lady's shoulders, it also credits her with the clever stratagem to turn chivalric ideals on themselves in the service of eros. She stages the contradictions of courtly love for her benefit; the knight appears merely to suffer from them.

The wider reaction to the knight's release as Erec defeats him suggests just how fraught the tensions between eros and adventure are for the society that Chrétien imagines. Finally, we understand why the episode is known as the Joy of the Court: Erec's liberation of the knight brings profound happiness to all, and people rush to the garden from all corners of the kingdom to celebrate. Presumably, the fellow's own ignominy is counteracted by the appearance of another knight, strong enough to trump eros. Yet just when the reader has accepted the general perspective on events, Chrétien reintroduces the other side of the coin: "Erec truly had his fill of joy and was well served according to his wishes, but it was far from pleasing to the woman who was sitting upon the silver bed" (113). The lady is eventually comforted by recognizing Enide as her cousin, but not before she drives home that the triumph of chivalry has necessarily led to the distress of a woman, ostensibly cherished and protected according to that same ideology. This contest is a zero-sum game: if the court takes its joy and the knight regains his freedom, it is because the lady has lost the constant presence of her lover.

The Joy of the Court episode, and the adulterous love of Lancelot and Guinivere, and Tristan and Iseult, show how eros complicates both feudal bonds and the knight's striving for martial honor. As in these central examples, the romance portrayal of courtly love often privileges the tensions and contradictions that shadow eros in the court – tensions between male and female perspectives, feudal and erotic bonds, personal and public imperatives. Yet occasionally eros may be presented in a less conflicted fashion, neatly aligned in the service of dynastic, licit reproduction, as in the uxorious version of Aeneas' story in the twelfth-century *Roman d'Eneas*, which I discuss below.

In general, however, romance is associated with illicit or threatening union. In fact, the texts themselves are characterized early on as erotic go-betweens. One of the most famous examples of this metaliterary recognition is the Paolo and Francesca episode in Dante's *Inferno* (1321). Francesca relates how she was led to adultery with her brother-in-law through their shared reading of an Arthurian romance:

> One day, to pass the time away, we read
> of Lancelot – how love had overcome him.
> We were alone, and we suspected nothing.
>
>   And time and time again that reading led
> our eyes to meet, and made our faces pale,
> and yet one point alone defeated us.

> When we had read how the desired smile
> was kissed by one who was so true a lover,
> this one, who never shall be parted from me,
> while all his body trembled, kissed my mouth.
> A Gallehault indeed, that book and he
> who wrote it, too; that day we read no more.
>   (Dante 1980: V.127–38)

The story of Lancelot and Guinivere's illicit union produces a kind of reverse mimesis as Paolo and Francesca reproduce the action in the text. The romance – and its author – become go-betweens, much like the Gallehault [Galahad] who encouraged the royal lovers. In Italian, the very word *galeoto* came to mean procurer.

A similar etymology lies behind the English *pander*, derived from the character Pandarus in Chaucer's *Troilus and Criseyde* (1382–5), based on Boccaccio's *Filostrato*. Chaucer embroiders a long narrative out of minor characters and details in various accounts of the Trojan War, and develops his sources into a full-scale exploration of sexual and political agency. Despite his ultimate condemnation of Criseyde, Chaucer offers us an unprecedented insight into her consciousness, as she debates her choices and cannily evaluates the limitations of her position. Chaucer's Pandarus is more than a mere go-between. As Sheila Fisher argues, he virtually genders the protagonists, encouraging Troilus into a more active masculinity than the conventions of courtly love afford him and transforming Criseyde into an object of exchange (Fisher 2000: 156). After conniving to bring the lovers together in Criseyde's chamber, Pandarus, in mock discretion, retires to a corner and pretends to be about to look into a romance, all while presumably watching the couple. This highly reflexive moment, cited in this chapter's epigraph, indicates a generic self-awareness of romance as the textual apparatus that slows history into eros.

ROMANCING ANTIQUITY

The reworked stories of Greece and Rome, such as *Troilus and Criseyde*, are the clearest example of romance as an operation of translation and transformation. The romances of antiquity are much more than a rendition in the vernacular; they adapt, expand, and transform the original texts in signal ways. The self-conscious transformation from Latin to the vernacular features, as I have suggested, a more sustained investigation of eros and a "playful and willfully anachronistic habit of comparing, contrasting, or directly inserting contemporary places, times, and institutions" within the time of the text (Baswell 2000: 32–3). This anachronism, Christopher Baswell argues, provides "a comparatively safe space within ancient story" in which to discuss medieval problems. It serves to probe contemporary society or challenge its values, while at the same time domesticating the classical world. More importantly, in telling a story that connects *then* and *now*, anachronistic romances grant contemporary modes of power an ancient or mythical validation (Baswell 2000: 32–3), identifying medieval monarchs, in particular, as descendants of Aeneas and putative heirs of Rome. These borrowed and transformed stories from the classical past thus constitute a central strategy for medieval Christendom's construction of its origins and history.

Chrétien de Troyes' own pen name – a Christian from Troy – suggests medieval romance's deep investment in a dual historical and cultural perspective: his is a Christian world-view, yet his cultural roots lie in the classical world of Greece and Rome. (Troyes is also a town in Northern France, but the classical echoes of the name are inescapable. For an account of the debates about Chrétien as historical figure or "author function," see Kay 1997.) Some critics view this as a dilemma: how can a Christian author imitate pagan texts (Dragonetti 1980: 20–2)? Yet as the romances of antiquity attest, the paradox seems to have been a fruitful one for twelfth-century humanism.

Medieval Christendom conceptualizes the connection between the classical past and the contemporary world in two important and related ways, both of which are prominently featured in the romances. The idea of *translatio studii* refers to the transfer of knowledge from the classical world to medieval Europe; *translatio imperii* to the migration of imperial power from Greece or Troy to Rome and its European inheritors. The clerk occupies a privileged role in the transfer of knowledge: as the prologue to Benoît de Sainte-Maure's *Roman de Troie* (c. 1160–5) explains, learning is preserved through the transmission and dissemination of knowledge (Benoît 1987: 35). The prologue to Chrétien's *Cligés*, which is set both in Arthur's court and in Greece, strikes a slightly different note: it first stresses the value of the story by underscoring its ancient provenance, then disdains the importance of past civilizations when compared to the present of France:

> The book containing the true story is very old, therefore it is all the more worthy of belief. Through the books we have, we learn of the deeds of ancient peoples and of bygone days. Our books have taught us that chivalry and learning first flourished in Greece; then to Rome came chivalry and the sum of knowledge, which now has come to France. May God grant that they be maintained here and may He be pleased enough with this land that the glory now in France may never leave. God merely lent it to the others: no one speaks any more of the Greeks or Romans; their fame has grown silent and their glowing ember has gone out.
>
> (Chrétien 1991: 123)

The references to glory suggest that the categories of knowledge and power tend to collapse into each other; although the narrator is only explicitly discussing the former, his choice of words as he worries about the transience of *translatio* indicates a concern with the latter. The multiple sites of vernacular literary production validate Chrétien's concern: will the westward march of empire and the mantle of Rome rest in France or in England? Or will they in fact proceed elsewhere?

The Virgilian legend of Aeneas' flight from Troy to Italy to found Rome serves as the primary conduit for *translatio imperii*. Geoffrey of Monmouth's extraordinarily influential Latin chronicle, the *Historia Regum Britanniae* (*History of the Kings of Britain*, c. 1138) linked the mythical founding of Britain to Troy and Rome through Brutus, Aeneas's grandson, and thus connected Arthur himself to the Roman imperial line. Wace's *Roman de Brut* (c. 1155) popularized the story in a vernacular version that also introduced Arthur's famous Round Table and its knights. Whether through their blatant anachronism or through the workings of *translatio*, therefore, the romances of antiquity are never far removed from contemporary concerns.

The translation of romance from the classical to the contemporary world is often reflected in the implicit logic of romance compilations that start with Troy and gradually move to Arthurian matter. One notable manuscript begins with the *Roman de Troie*, the story of the Trojan war, and then traces the story of Aeneas (*Roman d'Eneas*) through his descendants (*Roman de Brut*) to the foundation of Britain and the reign of King Arthur, an account supplemented by Chrétien's five Arthurian romances (Huot 2000: 63–4). Here, in a single manuscript, is the imaginative trajectory that undergirds much of medieval romance production.

How exactly does the "translation" of a classical text into a romance framework differ from its "original"? One key example is the *Roman d'Eneas* (c. 1155), which significantly alters its Latin model to emphasize the love story between Aeneas and Lavinia. In Virgil's *Aeneid*, Lavinia is a minor character with no voice of her own. Love appears primarily as a threat to empire, in Aeneas' ill-fated detour in Dido's Carthage. In the *Eneas*, by contrast, the story of Dido is a foil to the even more extensive account of Lavine's love for Eneas (to give them their French names) and his corresponding infatuation. Lavine may enable a proper dynastic alliance between Eneas and the native Laurentians, but she is also a maiden inflamed by love. The union between the two is overdetermined, with the erotic connection confirming and smoothing over the agreed transfer of power. Lavine's parents are explicit about the stakes of the marriage: King Latinus promises simultaneously to "give over my land to [Eneas] and make him the gift of my daughter" (*Eneas* 1974: 120), while Queen Amata, who longs to give her daughter to Turnus, as had originally been agreed, warns Lavine that Eneas vies for her "more for the land than for love of you" (*Eneas* 1974: 210).

Critics have connected the new emphasis on dynastic succession in the romance to the twelfth-century transformation of aristocratic clans into narrower "agnatic" structures – familial dynasties descending through the male line (Baswell 2000: 34–5). In this context, the yoking of a love story to dynastic succession makes perfect sense. Eros no longer works against empire, as in Virgil's original version, where Dido's threat is much more significant than Lavinia's promise; instead, it serves to cement alliances and ensure the survival and continuity of power. The emphasis on lineage also explains why the worst accusation that Amata can come up with to discourage her daughter, in another striking departure from Virgil, is that Eneas is a sodomite who prefers men to women: "It would quickly be the end of this life if all men were thus throughout the world. Never would a woman conceive; there would be a great dearth of people; no one would ever bear children, and the world would fail before a hundred years"

(*Eneas* 1974: 210). Amata's plea clearly reveals the familial, dynastic stakes in Lavine's marriage.

Despite these explicit acknowledgements of the union's strategic value, the narrative nonetheless superimposes a love story on the bare power struggles. Strikingly, while Eneas aggressively wars with Turnus for Lavine's hand and all that goes with it, Lavine is the instigator where their love is concerned. She engages in a lengthy dialogue with herself, describing her conflicted feelings and her subjection to love. This extended portrait of the lover's consciousness is a significant departure from Virgil, and from the preoccupations of epic. Instead, it anticipates the lengthy debates on love in Chrétien and Andreas Capellanus. It is at once intensely personal and peppered with commonplaces that give it the flavor of a courtly conduct book: "He who loves truly cannot deceive; he is loyal and cannot change" (*Eneas* 1974: 219–20). Tormented by love, Lavine finally decides to reveal her passion to Eneas, through a letter placed on an arrow shot into his camp. The arrow furthers both the love plot and the conflict: it effectively destroys the fragile truce between the two sides even as Eneas reciprocates Lavine's love.

Yet while the war comes to an end with Eneas' victory over Turnus, the love plot continues, as the reader is teased with yet another delay. Much to Lavine's dismay, instead of claiming her immediately, Eneas names a date eight days hence. Lavine's lament, and Eneas' own as he realizes how painful the delay will be to him, prolong the love plot for another three hundred lines. Erotic delay literally produces the text, made up entirely of the lovers' plaints. Lavine once again doubts whether Eneas loves her: "Now it seems to him, since he has won, that he has gained everything through the battle, and indeed he thinks that he will have dominion without me" (*Eneas* 1974: 252). Eneas, tossing and turning, berates himself: "What have I done, sorrowful wretch, that I have set such a distant date to have my beloved and take her? I can never wait so long. The time must be much shortened, for waiting is not easy for me. An hour of one day is longer than a year!" (*Eneas* 1974: 253). Despite the alignment of love with empire, that is, erotic delay still functions as a narrative strategy to provide suspense and pleasure, as in the classical romances discussed in Chapter 1. As medieval romance becomes more elaborate, narrative delays will become increasingly sophisticated, with the interlacing of multiple characters and plot lines.

CHIVALRY AND ADVENTURE

> Gawain put on good cheer.
> "Why should I hesitate?"
> He said. "Kind or severe,
> We must engage our fate."
> *Sir Gawain and the Green Knight*

With Eneas and his men behaving like medieval barons and Arthur's lineage linked to Troy, it seems difficult to distinguish between the "matter of Rome" and the "matter of Britain"; both take on the hallmarks of chivalry. The Arthurian material has had a peculiar hold on the popular imagination; in fact, one might argue that for most readers romance is synonymous with tales of chivalric adventure, of knights on a quest. Chrétien is largely responsible for the immense popularity of this material; one editor calls him "the inventor of Arthurian literature as we know it" (Chrétien 1991: 1). Although Chrétien found his material in legends, in Geoffrey of Monmouth, and in Wace's *Brut*, he added crucial components to the story: Guinevere's adulterous affair with Lancelot, the setting at Camelot, the adventures of the Grail (Chrétien 1991: 1). Chrétien's version of these stories was widely imitated in ever longer renditions, including, in the German tradition, Wolfram von Eschenbach's *Parzival* (c. 1205–12). The rewritings of Chrétien culminate in the enormous thirteenth-century prose compendium that brought together two of his central themes: the Lancelot-Graal (1225–50). The Vulgate Cycle, as it is also known, itself became the basis for Malory's *Morte d'Arthur* (1469–70), which continued to influence English literature long after Chrétien himself had fallen out of favor.

Arthurian literature owes its great popularity to a number of factors. It generally appealed to royal readers and their followers, and therefore prospered along with strong rulers. Conversely, in such powerful regional texts as *Sir Gawain and the Green Knight*, it could also stage the come-uppance of the court, in this case through the encounter of its bewildered representative with a massively powerful local lord and his knowing wife. Although the myth of Arthur was actively employed by English kings (particularly the later Tudor dynasty) to underscore their legitimacy and illustrious heritage, the Arthurian corpus also provides the *frisson* of the anti-monarchical through betrayals and challenges to the King's power, and often casts political problems such as succession, consensus, and loyalty in a magical or marvelous vein.

In formal terms, the expansive device of the Round Table, with its multiple cast of knights, proves singularly flexible and productive: there is always another knight to follow, another adventure to recount. Thus the Arthurian corpus enables the iterative quality of romance, since writers may return again and again to the same material, using the Round Table as a literal point of departure for their own narratives. Over several centuries and multiple versions, the overarching narrative absorbs powerful stories that are not logically connected to Arthur: Tristan and Iseult, the quest for the Holy Grail, and so forth. In chivalric romance, the court grounds the individual knight's wandering in search of adventures or his response to a mysterious challenge. It frames the open-ended or obscure excursions with the relative clarity of relationships and identities in the feudal center. In a classic study, Erich Auerbach argues that what distinguishes the romance knight from the warrior of the *chansons de geste* is the unmotivated nature of his excursion: "[The romance knight] sets out without mission or office; he seeks adventure, that is, perilous encounters by which he can prove his mettle. There is nothing like this in the *chanson de geste*. There a knight who sets off has an office and a place in a politico-historical context" (Auerbach 1953: 133). Even this relatively unmotivated agency, however, contrasts markedly with the Greek romances discussed in Chapter 1: in the medieval narratives, adventures sometimes befall the protagonists; more often, however, they are sought out or at least embraced, and then glorified through the appearance of marvels (Nerlich 1987: 5, 12). Recent criticism, in the wake of Jameson's seminal essay discussed in the Introduction (Jameson 1975), has recovered the historical import of romance as a genre that considers everything from the weakness of monarchs to the threat of civil war to the place of women in society. Although this newer criticism is an important corrective to Auerbach's formalism, it is undeniable that romance often presents a peculiar vagueness: relatively weak motivations and underdeveloped causality to undergird action; a fantastical setting that combines the contemporary and the antique, the familiar and the exotic; a deliberate emphasis on mystery and the active disguise of identity and points of reference; a disorienting flatness, with no privileging of one episode over another, of the fantastic over the realistic, or vice versa. Yet, as Heng has shown, these characteristics do not preclude romance's role as a crucible of cultural fantasy (Heng 2003: 3 and passim).

Chivalric romance develops a series of formal traits that accommodate its multiple plot lines and protagonists. At the most basic level, the narrative is segmented into sequential, self-contained episodes – Frye's "and then" narrative (Frye 1976: 47–9). A more sophisticated technique is the *interlace*, where different strands of the narrative are woven together. In a fascinating essay, Eugene Vinaver traces the visual equivalent of interlace in Romanesque ornament, which features entwined, knotted, and plaited "threads" (Vinaver 1971, 77–80). In the textual version, each plot is interrupted to advance the others. Interlace (formal causality) displaces motivation (logical causality) and, especially in the large romance cycles, becomes the structural device that organizes disparate episodic narratives. Thus, as Matilda Bruckner suggests, interlace "offers a potential commentary on the characters, episodes, or narrative segments juxtaposed and woven together" (Bruckner 2000: 25). In the more sophisticated instances, the interruption comes at a point of great suspense, and the narrator only returns to the previous narrative when the reader has become fully engrossed by the subsequent one. Interlace is one of the most fruitful formal contributions of medieval romance, and is consistently exploited by writers, from the Renaissance romance-epic to the twentieth-century comic book ("Meanwhile, back at the Hall of Justice . . .") and other popular genres.

ROMANCE GENRES

> At the end of the day, romance is, after all, the name of a desiring narrational modality that coalesces from the extant cultural matrix at hand, poaching and cannibalizing from a hybridity of all and any available resources, to transact a magical relationship with history, of which it is in fact a consuming part.
>
> Heng, *Empire of Magic*, 9

As we have seen, the term *romance* referred in medieval times to many different kinds of texts. Even though medieval studies has developed an artificial sense of romance as a genre, the corpus includes prose and verse, different lengths and subject matters, and so forth. Nonetheless, as Heng has recently argued, chivalric romance, due to its great popularity, is often taken synecdochically to stand in for all kinds of romance (Heng 2003: 4). Heng argues instead for an expansive sense of romance, comprising everything from chronicle histories to travelers' tales, and identified by "the structure of desire which powers its narrative, and the transformational repetition of that structure through innumerable variations" (Heng 2003: 3). Her broad category brings to the fore the "contamination" of multiple genres by romance that medievalists have long acknowledged. It suggests that even for this period we may posit romance as a set of mobile, adaptable strategies for making texts pleasurable. Idealization, narrative delays, multiple obstacles to teleological drives, spectacular reversals of fortune, constant use of the marvelous, a more pronounced role for eros: these romance strategies make their appearance in a wide variety of medieval genres, even in chronicle histories that are not "romanced" or translated into the vernacular.

This instrumental sense of romance allows modern readers to reconstruct the implicit dialogue between many different kinds of medieval texts, and even between texts and the larger culture that surrounds them. It restores the connections between romance as a circumscribed genre, venerated by generations of medievalists, and the richer panoply of popular or folk texts in a more broadly conceived cultural arena. The larger sense of romance reveals, for example, the similarities between certain hagiographic and chivalric texts, equally concerned with idealization; with naming and identity; and with loss, recognition, and restitution (Kay 1997: 14–19). It also explains why so many authors of "romances" appear to have written in a wide variety of genres: the strategies that often characterize their production are not necessarily circumscribed by traditional literary categories.

Heng's central case in point is the English canon Geoffrey of Monmouth's *Historia Regum Britanniae* (*History of the Kings of Britain*, c. 1138) which challenges the definition of romance even as it exhibits many of its elements. Geoffrey precedes the ur-texts of Chrétien, writes in Latin instead of *romanz*, and "invokes the authenticatory apparatus of historical narration, complete with the citation of earlier historical sources, provision of chronologies, onomastic and geographical descriptions, and a scrupulously causal and sequential recitation of Britain's past" (Heng 2003: 18).

Nonetheless, as critics have long recognized, there is much romance material in the *Historia*. In a controversial argument, Heng proposes that what characterizes Geoffrey as romance is precisely "the articulation of fantasy and history . . . as varieties of cultural work" that rescue its readership from the "communal trauma" of European atrocities in the First Crusade (Heng 2003: 18). Through a careful comparison of Crusade narratives, Heng argues that the fantastical episode in which Arthur confronts a cannibalistic giant at Mont Saint-Michel actually recalls *European* cannibalism in the East, transforming it into a fantastical figure of monstrosity that the hero can lay to rest. Thus, she observes, romance inhabits historical texts as a way both to surface and to contain ideological crises.

Romance also characterizes genres that ostensibly value moral utility over pleasure. Hagiography, the stories of saints' lives, presents multiple formal and structural similarities to what is traditionally considered the romance genre (Vinaver 1971: 111). Many of the most popular hagiographic narratives are vernacular – that is, *romance* – versions of Latin originals, much as the "romances of antiquity" are versions of classical texts. These saints' lives often emphasize adventure and high drama. By the thirteenth century, when vernacular literature was well established, hagiographers foreground the pleasure afforded by their stories, as well as the courtly excellence of their heroes. Most interestingly, their narratives depend on some of the same strategies as the courtly texts traditionally classified as romances: the idealization of the protagonist; the amplification of travails as a series of adventures; the tension between desire and the protagonist's quest. Rather than critiquing the immorality of romance, as Renaissance moralists later did, hagiographers harness its strategies to enliven their own narratives. "Heroic sanctity," as Brigitte Cazelles aptly terms it (Cazelles 1991: 24), depends on a refusal of the earthly in favor of the spiritual, and yet the textual dynamics are strikingly similar to those of chivalric narratives in which a knight must learn to choose virtue over temptation, or refuse eros for the sake of adventure. The most interesting difference, I would suggest, is that the hagiographic corpus offers many more female protagonists. Their chastity, resourcefulness, and versatility often recall the heroines of Byzantine romances, such as Chariclea, who are given shape by their sufferings and resistance. In the *Life of Saint Faith*, written by Simon of Walsingham c. 1210, for example, the heroine's beauty initially moves her tormentor Dacian to pity, and he lasciviously redirects her to "the goddess of love":

> Beautiful maiden,
> Endowed with such grace
> And such youth,
> Stop here this madness!
> Abandon this religion,
> Which is nothing but nonsense,
> And go offer sacrifice
> And prayers to Saint Diana.
> You must honor her,
> The goddess of love.
> Believe me and adore her,
> Who shares with you the same nature.
>
> (Cazelles 1991: 190)

Faith is unswayed by the Roman officer. Strikingly, the narrative harnesses the prurience of his gaze to provide a voyeuristic, sadistic pleasure for the audience through the description of her torture:

> Saint Faith is then disrobed
> And laid upon the bed.
> The naked maiden
> Is tied down.
> Her frail body is stretched
> By those who hate God's friends.
> Upon Dacian's order,
> A fire is kindled under her.
> The cruel soldiers light it
> With burning rods.
> The fire is fed with grease,
> Thrown in the flames by these evil men,
> Who kindle the fire in this way.
> Above it is the maiden,
> Frail and helpless.
> She is soon engulfed by the fire.
>
> (Cazelles 1991: 192)

As Faith is literally consumed by her Passion, the reader also consumes the depiction of her vulnerable, naked body. Despite its moralistic intentions, that is, hagiography often trades in textual pleasure, much as the lay romances.

It is important to note that the connections between hagiography and chivalric literature are reciprocal: saintly protagonists are secularized, while knights strive for spiritual ideals (Cazelles 1991: 31). The immense popularity of the Grail legend demonstrates the particular force of these combinations. Cazelles notes that later versions of saints' lives often attempt to harness the power of "romance" as explicitly as possible (Cazelles 1991: 32). Cazelles names the resulting genre "hagiographic romance," yet the romance qualities exceed any particular generic classification. It is useful instead to contemplate what kinds of techniques and topoi – the instrumental sense of romance – animate a wide variety of medieval narratives.

Another fascinating set of narratives that depend on romance strategies are the *Lais* of the poet Marie de France (c. 1170–80). As a genre, the *lay* is sometimes considered a subset of romance, yet is generally contrasted with the traditional romance in terms of length: critics sometimes describe it as a kind of "snapshot" or episode extracted from the fuller narrative sweep of a proper romance. Yet what seems most striking is the extent to which the *lais* share the preoccupations of the romance genre, and evince some of the same romance strategies – such as idealization, postponement, the tension between the martial and the erotic – though often with a decidedly feminist twist. It is almost as though they were the obverse of the more masculine chivalric literature, presenting not exactly the world of women but the world of chivalry as experienced by women. At times, the *lais* are wonderfully self-conscious, commenting explicitly on the strategies they recognize or eschew, and ironizing the recognizable clichés of chivalric and courtly literature in their abbreviated form. *Guigemar*, for example, features a painting of Venus "casting into a blazing fire the book in which Ovid teaches the art of controlling love and as excommunicating all those who read this book or adopted its teachings" (Marie 1999: 46). The *lay* contrasts convoluted Ovidian machinations with the simplicity of true love, as the knight urges the lady to move beyond convention and grant him her favors immediately:

> "My lady," he replied, "in God's name, have mercy on me! Do not be distressed if I say this: a woman who is always fickle likes to extend courtship in order to enhance her own esteem and so that the man will not realize that she has experienced the pleasure of love. But the well-intentioned lady, who is worthy and wise, should not be too harsh towards a man, if she finds him to her liking; she should rather love him and enjoy his love. Before anyone discovers or hears of their love, they will greatly profit from it. Fair lady, let us put an end to this discussion." The lady recognized the truth of his words and granted him her love without delay.
>
> (Marie 1999: 50)

The pointedly brief exchange pokes fun at not only the longueurs of romance delay but also the love casuistry that characterizes so much of medieval writing on eros. Later, the same *lay* ironically reminds us of the generalizing effect of romance hyperbole: Guigemar thinks that he recognizes his beloved in a beautiful lady but cannot be certain, given that "women look very much alike" (Marie 1999: 53).

Chaitivel is entirely constructed around the ironic dismantling of romance idealization, and recalls Gawain's objection to the beauty contest in *Erec and Enide*. In the *lay*, a lady finds herself unable to choose among the knights who inevitably fall in love with her:

> It was not possible for her to love them all, but neither did she wish to repulse them. It would be less dangerous for a man to court every lady in an entire land than for a lady to remove a single besotted lover from her skirts, for he will immediately attempt to strike back.
>
> (Marie 1999: 105)

Initially, the *lay* playfully considers the pressures that eros places on the beloved, instead of lingering on the more usual suffering of the lover. The irony is pronounced: the four principal suitors are so ideal that "no one could distinguish between them in any way" (Marie 1999: 106). Finally a tournament is called, in which three of the knights die while the fourth receives a deep wound in the thigh. The lady decides to channel her sorrow into a *lay* entitled "The Four Sorrows" that will tell the story of her four lovers. In a metaliterary moment, the surviving knight argues for his own preeminence, if only in his ongoing suffering:

"My lady, compose the new lay, but call it *The Unhappy One*. I shall explain why it should have this title. The others have long since ended their days and used up their span of life. What great anguish they suffered on account of the love they bore for you! But I who have escaped alive, bewildered and forlorn, constantly see the woman I love more than anything on earth, coming and going; she speaks to me morning and evening, yet I cannot experience the joy of a kiss or an embrace or of any pleasure other than conversation. You cause me to suffer a hundred such ills and death would be preferable for me. Therefore the lay will be named after me and called *The Unhappy One*. Anyone who calls it *The Four Sorrows* will be changing its true name." "Upon my word," she replied, "I am agreeable to this: let us now call it *The Unhappy One*."

(Marie 1999: 108)

The knight's plea reveals a perverse truth about romance (recall the hagiographies discussed above): it often measures excellence in terms of the capacity for suffering. Yet the irony of the lover's situation is also inescapable: instead of rewarding him when there is no one left to compete for her attention, the lady is now grief-stricken and consumed with mourning. She agrees to change the name of the *lay*, but not to assuage his erotic suffering. Given the thigh wound, one could read the knight as physically disabled and deprived of love, yet his specific mention of how he cannot experience even a kiss or an embrace suggests that the problem lies in the lady's unwillingness. Thus erotic consummation is endlessly postponed, displaced here into an irresolvable literary discussion, for the new name for the *lay* fails to stick:

Thus was the lay begun, and later completed and performed. Some of those who put it into circulation call it *The Four Sorrows*. Each name is appropriate and supported by the subject matter. It is commonly known as *The Unhappy One*. Here it ends, for there is no more. I have heard no more, know no more and shall relate no more to you.

(Marie 1999: 108)

After noting for the reader how texts sometimes escape the control of those who produce them, the narrator exercises her power to withhold the pleasure of textual consummation. There is no certainty; there is no more.

Instead of consummation and pleasure, the dilation of the lover's patient erotic penance ends with the narrator's deliberate manipulation of romance expectations.

If we take romance in this more expansive sense, it penetrates even where we might not expect it, such as into pure lyric. Although the notion of romance as a narrative strategy of delay seems to make little sense for lyric, an individual poem or series may well recreate the romance sense of error and wandering. Perhaps the most powerful example of this is Petrarch's sequence, the *Rime sparse* or scattered rhymes, a collection of vernacular lyric poems, written 1330–74, that both contemplates and enacts amatory delay. Taken as a whole, the sequence traces the sustained unattainability of the beloved, and the poet's erring in love. A particularly striking example of what we might call the romance lyric is poem 189, which I transcribe in Robert Durling's translation:

My ship laden with forgetfulness passes through a harsh sea, at
midnight, in winter, between Scylla and Charybdis, and at the
tiller sits my lord, rather my enemy;

each oar is manned by a ready, cruel thought that seems to scorn

the tempest and the end; a wet, changeless wind of sighs, hopes, and
desires breaks the sail;

a rain of weeping, a mist of disdain wet and loosen the already weary
ropes, made of error twisted up with ignorance.

My two usual sweet stars are hidden; dead among the waves are
reason and skill; so that I begin to despair of the port.

(Petrarch 1976: 334)

Although this vernacular lyric clearly cannot share the narrative thrust of romance-as-genre, it conjures up many of the larger romance strategies that I have identified: the unaccomplished voyage, interrupted by error and wandering, is animated by an erotic desire that both produces subjectivity and casts the protagonist – in this case, the lyric "I" – into conflict with himself. The sonnet even recalls romance predecessors, invoking Scylla and Charybdis. Thus Petrarch's lyric, even at the level of the individual sonnet, may be said to deploy romance, in the instrumental, strategic sense that I have been proposing, as a kind of textual template for productive longing, the delay that paradoxically yields text.

Medieval romance, whether as the traditional genre or in the expanded sense of strategy that I have presented here, is an enormous field. Though this chapter covers a large range, it can by no means do justice to the huge corpus that could be considered under this rubric. Given the striking interpenetrability of medieval genres, moreover, the category of romance is constantly shifting and expanding. This movement is even more pronounced as romance becomes increasingly sophisticated and self-referential, spawning sequels and rewritings both long before print culture and in the first age of print. In this sense, we should perhaps speak of how these iterable and iterated texts participate in or draw on romance, instead of categorizing them as individual instances.

Beyond proposing the expansion of genre into strategy, it is important to dispel certain easy categorizations of romance. As the readings of Chrétien and Marie de France show, romance may easily reconcile idealization with devastating irony, the marvelous and magic with penetrating realism. Similarly, its desirous wish-fulfillment and emphasis on individual quests by no means place it outside history; if anything, as Heng argues, romance becomes a particularly effective tool for inter-mingling history and collective fantasy. Romance confronts us with the paradoxes of narrative. While there is an undeniable misogyny and sadism in its frequent association of eros with delay, and its subjection of both heroes and heroines to endless tests and trials, these obstacles turn out to be wildly productive in narratological terms: they literally make the story, and in the process often construct the subjectivity of their protagonists.

3

ROMANCE IN THE RENAISSANCE

THE (RE)INVENTION OF ROMANCE

As the vernacular literature of the Renaissance enters into a rich conversation with its classical and medieval antecedents, romance is extensively refashioned into a range of new possibilities. The Greek romances, rediscovered in the sixteenth century, are widely translated and imitated. The novella tradition, from Boccaccio to his multiple imitators, builds on a number of romance strategies and provides many of the plots for Renaissance drama. Central figures such as Ariosto, Spenser, Tasso, and Cervantes elaborate on the tradition of medieval romance, deconstruct classical epic by exposing and questioning its conventions, and constantly engage in generic play. In the theoretical debates about the nature and value of romance, as well as in the texts debated, one can trace the origins of its conceptualization as a literary strategy of pleasurable multiplicity, opposed to the single-mindedness and political instrumentality of epic. That is, whereas epic is most often associated with stories of effective quests, corporate achievement, and the heroic birth of nations, romance challenges these narratives by privileging instead the wandering hero, the erotic interlude, or the dangerous delay.

David Quint explains this opposition, so central to the literary history of the Renaissance, through the figure of the enchanted boat. In chivalric romance, he claims:

> such ships embody the adventure principle that is a ubiquitous, perhaps essential feature of romance narrative: counterbalancing an equally constitutive quest principle, it accounts for all the digressions and subplots which delay the quest's conclusion and which come to acquire an attraction and validity of their own . . . In epic narrative, which moves to a predetermined end, the magic ship signals a digression from a central plot line, but the boat of romance, in its purest form, has no other destination than the adventure at hand. It cannot be said to be off course. New adventures crop up all the time, and the boat's travels describe a romance narrative that is open-ended and potentially endless.
>
> (Quint 1985: 179)

Despite his insistence on the difference between romance and epic, Quint acknowledges the presence of the former in the latter. The best way to understand this tension is to recognize romance as a strategy that occurs in many different kinds of texts, and that has a particularly productive role within epic.

The Italian Renaissance produced sophisticated, complex instances of the strategic or instrumental sense of romance. Perhaps most dazzling is Ludovico Ariosto's *Orlando Furioso* (1516, 1532). The poem is based on the martial, epic tradition of the *matière de France*, the heroic medieval narratives about Roland, the great knight of Charlemagne who helped his king resist the Saracens. The most famous of these narratives was the eponymous, eleventh-century *Chanson de Roland*, but the tradition of the heroic Roland was widespread. The *Furioso*, with its hero gone mad for love, counters its predecessors by foregrounding a multiplicity of satiric and erotic plots. Ariosto follows in the footsteps of his predecessor, Matteo Boiardo, who had already romanced the warrior by having him fall in love with the elusive Eastern princess Angelica in his sprawling, unfinished *Orlando Innamorato* (1483, 1494). Ariosto returns to Boiardo's plot in a dazzling, highly self-conscious text that, from its opening lines, challenges the parameters of both epic and chivalric romance. The poet promises to sing "of knights and ladies, of love and arms, of courtly chivalry, of courageous deeds" (Ariosto 1974: 1.1). With a deliberate nod to the opening lines of Virgil's *Aeneid* ("I sing of arms and the man"), he raises ladies and love, which are central concerns of the romance tradition, to the same level as the epic pursuit of war. This concern with love will mark the signal Renaissance texts that combine epic and romance, and which themselves imitate Ariosto, such as Torquato Tasso's *Jerusalem Delivered* (1581) and Edmund Spenser's *The Faerie Queene* (1591, 1596). For all of these texts, the tension between martial quest and erotic detour will be a central organizing principle.

Ariosto's concern with female characters leads to one of the striking innovations of Renaissance epic: a hugely expanded role for the female knight. In Ariosto and in his followers, these characters, Bradamante, Marfisa, Clorinda, dress as men for most of the text and are, in some cases, only belatedly recognized as women. Although, for some, agency is circumscribed by an early death or a capitulation to marriage, their extended disguise, which results from choice rather than from necessity, complicates the gender politics of chivalric romance.

Ariosto acerbically exposes the inevitable contradictions of chivalry, and reminds the reader of its fundamental obsolescence in the age of gunpowder. Yet his poem nonetheless serves as a *summa* of the romance tradition, combining classical precedents such as the enchantress Alcina, based on Circe in the *Odyssey*, with a full cast of medieval marvels, such as magical weapons, giants, sorcerers, enchanted castles, and a formal tour de force of interlacing narratives that weave together multiple plots. The main strand traces the hero's fruitless quest for Angelica, whose union with the humble soldier Medoro drives Orlando mad. The deranged knight abandons his king, Charlemagne, at the height of the Saracen assault, and almost causes the fall of Paris. Orlando is finally restored by the knight Astolfo, who, in one of the most comically spectacular of romance quests, travels to the moon in search of the warrior's missing wits. Ariosto also invents an illustrious story of dynastic origins for his patrons, much as Virgil attempts to establish the retrospective legitimacy of Augustus in the *Aeneid*, and via a similar use of proleptic prophecy, fully accomplished in the reader's own time. Thus the female knight Bradamante and her beloved Ruggiero, the poem tells us, are destined to be founders of the house of Este, although she spends most of the poem haplessly searching for him while he is repeatedly distracted by other objects of desire. The dynastic motive is constantly ironized, particularly when Astolfo learns from no other than St John, scribe to Jesus himself, that writers manipulate the truth to suit their patrons. As Patricia Parker observes, "Romance in Ariosto is not only subjected to a thorough anatomy of its characteristic errancy – the sense that its potentially infinite digression and variety may be resistant to completion or authorial control; it also becomes a means of revealing the fictiveness and errancy of all literary forms, including epic and even Scripture" (Parker 1990: 615).

Ariosto's poem addresses the incompatibility of romance and epic: the conventions of the former, which involve magical voyages and heroes wandering off the field of battle in pursuit of a beautiful maiden or into some treacherously beguiling space, are precisely about evading the latter, while the irreverence of his tone belies the seriousness of heroic poetry. The matter-of-fact marvels of romance are constantly ironized: Ruggiero, for example, goes red in the face for shame at the unfair advantage his magic shield confers on him, and drops it in a well (Ariosto 1974: 22.90–4). More importantly, the *Furioso* underscores the contrast between the easy mobility of romance – the mobility of individuals across geographical borders but also between different religious or racial camps – and the obsessive concerns with separation and difference of the emerging early modern states. The wandering of romance occurs during a suspension of royal power and royal prerogatives, and of the individual's duty to his liege. Individual chivalric encounters while the heroes are away from the front do not observe the same rules as collective battles, so that the Christian knights occasionally experience love or friendship for the "infidels" whom they are collectively fighting. Thus romance challenges the political myth-making of epic, and its tight networks of obligation and belonging.

The capaciousness and wry waywardness of the *Furioso* foreground romance as an ideal strategy of narrative expansiveness, trumping the single-minded, collective purposefulness of epic with rich detours into individual experience, erotic delay, and the exploration of alternative perspectives. Yet Ariosto reveals a certain ambivalence about this suspension, as though in rueful recognition that narrative ultimately requires a return to a teleological or quest mode. Certain episodes stage this recognition in what we have come to perceive as a familiar romance maneuver, associating stasis or error with the female agents of eros. Damaged or emasculated warriors must be hauled back to the battlefield, as when Orlando's wits are restored, or Ruggiero is liberated from his blissful hiatus in Alcina's island. Note how the description of Ruggiero, effeminized and sinking in luxury, rehearses the Orientalist topoi of Aeneas in Dido's Carthage, the substance of Virgil's own version of epic derailed by romance:

> The delicious softness of his dress suggested sloth and sensuality; Alcina had woven the garment with her own hands in silk and gold, a subtle work./ A glittering, richly jeweled necklace fastened round his neck and hung to his chest, while his two arms, hitherto so virile, were now each clasped by a lustrous bangle. Each ear was pierced by a fine gold ring from which a fat pearl hung, such as no Arabian or Indian ever boasted./ His curly locks were saturated in perfumes, the most precious and aromatic that exist. His every gesture was mincing, as though he were accustomed to waiting on ladies in Valencia.
>
> (Ariosto 1974: 7.53–5)

A glance at Ariosto's predecessors allows us to place this episode squarely within the tradition of the emasculated warrior, who must be released from his sensual stasis to seek heroic realization.

Yet other episodes are more complex, serving as miniature versions of the poem's own dilatory, wayward movement. The wizard Atlas, who attempts to save Ruggiero from early death, devises an enchanted castle in which every character fruitlessly searches for his or her object of desire:

> They all complained about the malicious invisible lord of that palace – /the invisible lord for whom they were all searching. All accused him of one theft or another; one was grieving over the loss of his horse, another was raging over the loss of his lady; others had other thefts to charge him with, and none of them could tear themselves away from this cage – some there were, the victims of this deception, who had been there for whole weeks and months.
>
> (Ariosto 1974: 12.11–12)

Our poet has quite a lot in common with the malicious lord the knights complain of: he, too, has set his characters on frustrating quests for impossible objects. But Atlas' palace does not last long; Astolfo destroys it using a magical book that conveniently lists the enchanted palace in its index, that novel marvel of Renaissance book technology as magical as any spell. He then releases the knights to, presumably, more fruitful quests, or perhaps simply to continue the ones interrupted by the enchanted palace. Yet Ariosto is not done with romance wandering: in the very act of destroying the palace, Astolfo finds the winged Hippogryph, a swift and uncontrollable steed that diverts the plot in spectacular fashion, sending its riders further and further afield. More importantly, the reader comes to recognize that the outcome postponed by distractions, magical opponents, and other forms of romance delay is none other than death: Ruggiero's fated early demise, which Atlas attempts in vain to forestall, or Orlando's own death at Roncesvalles. This recognition lends a particular poignancy to the multiplicity and variety of romance, whose undecidability and unboundedness appear, in this light, as a reprieve from the finality of epic endings.

Although the *Furioso* predates the widespread circulation of Aristotle's *Poetics* in the 1530s, it became a major point of contention in the literary quarrels that followed. Ariosto's poem crystallized the *romanzo* for Italian critics such as Giraldi Cintio, who applauded its variety and multiplicity, and its pleasurable digressions. Thus the Renaissance produces yet another kind of origin for romance, codified and theorized in an extensive critical debate. Whereas some critics attempt to reconcile romance and classical epic, others emphasize the difference between them.

In his 1554 *I romanzi*, a full-fledged theory of romance as genre, Giovanni Battista Pigna attempts to reconcile the form with Aristotelian criteria, which privilege truth, unity, and singularity. While epic imitates truth, romance, like comedy, invents, yet treats "known or 'true'" subjects (Weinberg 1961: 445). Pigna develops a classical genealogy for romance by claiming that, like the *Odyssey*, it mixes "high" and "low" characters. Yet he betrays a certain anxiety about this multiplicity: "each romance will be such through a great variety of infinite fortunes, and in the rank of the persons it will also be of two kinds, but it will tend towards the highest rather than toward the lowest, and almost every one of its actions will be illustrious" (cited in Weinberg 1961: 445). Thus Pigna attempts to recover romance by making it almost as "high" as epic. Similar problems arise when he tries to theorize the right number of actions in a "multiple" plot: "The number is 'sufficient' when they have put the heroes in all those honorable perils and in all those major actions which are sought in a perfect knight; and in this way endless adventures are avoided" (cited in Weinberg 1961: 446). Pigna acknowledges, despite himself, the potential open-endedness of a form that embraces both multiplicity and idealization. Notably, he counters Aristotle in assigning central importance to the pleasure provided by romance, particularly by the romance marvelous, and in valorizing "variety, multiplicity, diversity, discontinuity" over structural unity (Weinberg 1961: 447).

The influential critic Giraldi Cintio, for his part, establishes Ariosto as the culmination of a new form. He breaks with classicism by emphasizing the contemporaneity of romance: if epic was an appropriate genre for Greeks and Romans, romance is equally appropriate for modern Italians, whose culture and literature are similarly influenced by French, Provençal, and Spanish traditions (Weinberg 1961: 960–1). Giraldi elevates Ariosto's romance, claiming it as the highest expression of a particularly Italian sensibility, "the majesty of our language and our nation," and insists that the *Furioso*'s widespread popularity is in itself proof of its greatness (cited in Weinberg 1961: 962). Although his position would be much disputed, Giraldi's relativism affords romance a hitherto unthinkable place in the cultural pantheon.

But whether romance is praised or criticized, its classification as a genre seems patently insufficient, given the constant combination and contamination of forms in the poems of Ariosto, Tasso, and Spenser. Romance cannot be quarantined into a generic category; instead, it infects other genres, particularly epic, as an often unwelcome, or at least vexed, strategy of errancy and multiplicity. Romance counters teleology – and the accompanying ideology of national or religious destiny – with a special kind of narrative entropy, often coded as the presence of the feminine or the religious/racial Other. The challenge for such texts is to harness the appeal of romance while retaining the order of epic.

It is precisely such romance entropy that Torquato Tasso attempts to contain in *Jerusalem Delivered* (1581), his endlessly rewritten and anxiously defended epic on the First Crusade. With varying degrees of success, Tasso weaves the various plot threads of a digressive crusade and its wandering protagonists into the main plot of singular Christian achievements against the infidel. Tasso deliberately sets out to resolve the problem of Ariosto as a hugely popular but comically subversive model. Although the balance is different, in Tasso's poem, as in Ariosto's, romance counters epic, disrupting the workings of political authority by simply ignoring it: the moments of romance are those when characters carry on as though there were no crusade to be fought, no Christian prince to be obeyed. Alternatively, one might read Tasso's poem as the forcible harnessing of romance to epic: chance adventure is recoded as the expression of Providence's will (Quint 1993: 248–53) and wayward characters are ultimately contained. The primary challenge of the poem is to recover the knight Rinaldo, whose errancy endangers the Christian struggle against the Saracens, much as Orlando's flight in the *Furioso* imperils the besieged Paris. He must not only be freed from his enthrallment to the enchantress Armida (another figure in the tradition of Circe, to whom she is explicitly compared [Tasso 1987: 4.86], and Ariosto's Alcina) but firmly subjected to the authority of the righteous, singular leader imagined by Tasso, Godfrey of Boulogne. As Timothy Hampton points out, Tasso's poem is particularly intent on transforming the individualistic, romance chivalric code with "a single-minded mode of action centered on the group" (Hampton 1990: 100–1).

Armida's plot to spirit away Godfrey's best warriors by appealing to him as a "wretched maiden, orphaned and innocent," (Tasso 1987: 4.61) in need of a champion to recover her usurped throne, patently stages the tensions between epic and romance. Tasso's text resounds with earlier instances of this dichotomy: when Godfrey appears unmoved by Armida's pleas, his knights echo Dido's condemnation of Aeneas' choice of epic teleology over romance diversion: "Each man shares her affliction and says to himself: 'If she does not get aid from Godfrey now, surely a raging tigress was his nurse and among rugged mountains the forbidding rock ridge brought him forth, or the wave that shatters itself and froths on the sea: cruel man, that distresses and destroys such beauty'" (Tasso 1987: 4.77). One young knight makes explicit Armida's appeal to individual chivalry: while "the principal men that are here in charge of their subordinate troops" cannot possibly abandon their obligations, the "soldiers of fortune, without any personal charges" must come to the aid of "the innocent virgin," lest "it be reported in France, or wheresoever courtesy is prized," that they have shunned her cause (Tasso 1987: 4.79–81).

Ultimately, although Godfrey himself resists her, the Eastern enchantress captivates his men, who abandon the corporate crusade for the individual pursuit of adventure, honor and eros. Armida guides them "by winding and unused ways" (Tasso 1987: 10.60) to her earthly paradise, where she imbues them with "a deep forgetfulness" (Tasso 1987: 10.65) and transforms them into animals. But unlike the Circe episode of the *Odyssey*, in which animality simply reflects the men's debauchery, this enchantment occurs within the epic frame of conflict between Christians and Saracens, so that Armida offers to restore the knights if they will turn "pagan" (Tasso 1987: 10.69) and fight against Godfrey. Refusing, they are instead freed by Rinaldo, who himself falls prey to Armida.

The hero's approach bears all the hallmarks of romance. He parts company with his men to board a beckoning boat that announces a magical island: "O you, whoever you may be, whose will or fortune brings you to these waters in your wandering, not East nor West has greater marvels than that which the little island conceals. Pass over if you wish to see it" (Tasso 1987: 14.58). Nymphs call to Rinaldo to embrace pleasure and renounce glory and virtue. Seduced by Armida, he gladly does so, until two knights release him by showing him his debauched image reflected in a shield (Tasso 1987: 16.30). The break is not absolute, however: even though Armida echoes Dido in condemning Rinaldo, he promises to be her knight as long as it will not conflict with his martial obligation. And indeed, when the "pagans" are defeated, the two are reconciled, and Armida's own conversion to Christianity completes the rout.

Yet this final containment of romance by epic, after Armida's paradise has been destroyed, the knight restored, and the Christian victory assured, fails to convince. The conversion scene, which is a representation of Christian orthodoxy to replace the heterodox errancy of romance, is far from verisimilar, to use Tasso's own term (Fuchs 2001: 32). It happens at the eleventh hour, a mere eight stanzas before the end of the poem, as though the rush to right romance required last-minute transformations, however improbable. Moreover, the reader remains acutely aware of Armida's great powers of deception. In defeat, she considers her options, desperate but nonetheless recalling her powers: "Now what new art is left for me, or what new shape to which I might yet transform myself?" (Tasso 1987: 20.67). Might the wily enchantress, as Jane Tylus suggests, merely be parodying "the act of conversion, miming and thereby appropriating Christianity through her pagan craft?" (Tylus 1993: 107–8). The problem of Armida's conversion suggests the larger tensions that emerge when romance inhabits epic, as in Tasso's own conflicted poem. Even the most orthodox of texts cannot completely suppress the beguiling and ideologically compromised alternatives of romance.

In his poem, as in his theoretical writings, Tasso struggles constantly with the appeal of romance, evidenced in the phenomenal success of Ariosto's *Furioso*: multiplicity and the marvelous make for far more successful texts than Aristotelian unities and historical truth. One solution is to Christianize the marvelous into the *miraculous*: what may seem wondrous from a human perspective, Tasso argues, may be verisimilar when read as a manifestation of God's power (Rhu 1993: 103–4). Yet this counter-Reformation attempt to tame the marvelous by placing it in a theological context only risks greater unorthodoxy, by making the poet an opportunistic mimic of God's truth (Fuchs 2001: 26–7). Ultimately, Tasso cannot quite abandon the appeal of the romance marvelous, even though his attempts to contain it mire him in ever greater controversy. His oeuvre, both enlivened and burdened by eros and magic, evinces the incredible popularity and the conflicted reception of Renaissance romance.

Yet a different harnessing of romance to epic animates Spenser's *The Faerie Queene* (1591, 1596), which explicitly emulates Homer, Virgil, Ariosto, and Tasso. Spenser's project is patently national, his monumental contribution to a court culture that conceptualized the female sovereign as a Petrarchan lady, respectfully and hopelessly adored by her subject-suitors. Spenser dedicates his poem to Elizabeth, places her at the center of the text as the elusive Faerie Queene, and refracts her into other characters who allegorize her virtues. At the same time, however, the inclusion of several tyrannical "mayden Queene's" (Spenser 1978: I.4.8), such as Lucifera, Malecasta, or Radigund, suggests a more muted critique of female rule and of Elizabeth's stubborn refusal to marry. The announced hero of the poem is none other than the British Arthur, who by the late sixteenth century had been fully incorporated into Tudor monarchical propaganda. Spenser imagines him on a quest for the Faerie Queene, whom he has seen in a dream vision:

> From that day forth I cast in carefull mind,
> To seeke her out with labour, and long tyne,
> And neuer vow to rest, till her I find,
> Nine monethes I seeke in vaine yet ni'll that vow vnbind.
>
> (Spenser 1978: I.9.15)

In his prefatory "letter of the authors expounding his whole intention in the course of this worke," addressed to Sir Walter Raleigh, Spenser announces a classical, rational structure: twelve books of twelve cantos, each representing a knight's adventure, and all originating at the Faerie Queene's annual feast. The description of the feast itself, in Book XII, will cap the poem and retrospectively make sense of the disparate adventures.

Yet as any reader of *The Faerie Queene* knows, the actual structure of the poem is very different, and the individual quests are never ultimately achieved. Spenser published three books in 1590 and three more in 1596; the 1609 folio, which appeared after his death, appended two "Mutabilitie Cantos," plus two stanzas of a third, presumed to be part of the original design. The poem remains open-ended and inconclusive, with none of the structural clarity that the ambitious poet promises at the start. In fact, the Faerie Queene never appears in the text, complicating its centripetal, monarchical thrust. Instead, as the poet's letter itself admits, "many other aduentures are intermedled, but rather as Accidents, then intendments" (Spenser 1978: 18). In its episodic multiplicity, Spenser's text veers away from the single-mindedness of epic into the wandering of romance.

The formal ambiguity is reflected thematically, as the poem makes extensive use of the topoi of chivalric romance, with individual knights encountering individual enemies in a landscape full of marvels. Unlike Tasso or even Ariosto, Spenser does not place his characters in a historical context. Instead, they must be unpacked as allegories for their relevant political meanings. Ideology is filtered through a dense scrim of romance marvels; in Book I, for example, the Knight of Holiness, who is also George, patron saint of England, must help restore Una, the true Protestant Church, by defeating the apocalyptic dragon Errour. Yet as the poem proceeds the allegorical plots are increasingly interrupted by interlaced episodes that are harder to reconcile with the stated ethical project, "to fashion a gentleman or noble person in vertuous and gentle discipline" (Spenser 1978: 15). Particularly in Book III, the Legend of Britomart or Chastity, the pleasures of erotic dalliance threaten to undo exemplarity.

More generally, as Patricia Parker and Jonathan Goldberg have observed, the quest-like structure of the books, with one hero fulfilling one virtue, dissolves into endless deferral and multiplicity. Parker notes: "The poem's dilation by episode and digression stands in marked contrast to the straightforward linear progress of the pageants and 'triumphs' with which it is filled, and the reader must frequently seek understanding by more indirect routes" (Parker 1979: 70). The relatively distinct knights of Books I and II give way to fragmented appearances and a bewildering multiplication of characters. In Book III we have both Florimell and the False Florimell, and in Book IV the brothers Priamond, Diamond, and Triamond. Meanwhile, the ostensible heroes of each legend are further removed from the action. Goldberg argues that with such "radical disturbances of narration" the text "would seem to have abandoned entirely the assumption that plot moves character towards a goal, or that the protagonists embody theme" (Goldberg 1981: 6). Thus the pleasures of completion are replaced by the "endlesse worke" (Spenser 1978: IV.12.1) of displacement and deferral (Goldberg 1981: 8).

A key instance of this deferral, clearly revealed by the poem's textual history, lies in the final stanzas of Book III. In the 1590 version of the poem, the book culminates with the union of Scudamour and Amoret, perfectly joined in an idealized vision of "that faire Hermaphrodite" (Spenser 1978: III.12, 46a). The 1596 version radically challenges the satiety and stasis of this ending: the lovers miss each other, leading to the lady's "new affright," and changing the knight's expectation "to despaire" (Spenser 1978: III.12, 45–6). As Goldberg points out, "The deliberate cancelation of an ending carries with it an implicit assumption: that narration cannot progress beyond an ending – any ending" (Goldberg 1981: 1). Yet if the deferral provides endless narration, and "endlesse worke," it also complicates the possibility of any closure to the poem.

The "unperfite" ending of the 1609 text specifically addresses this concern. The Cantos of Mutabilitie feature the judgment of Mutabilitie by Nature. Although Mutabilitie appears to have the upper hand, Nature subsumes change to an overriding teleology:

> I well consider all that ye haue sayd
> And find that all things stedfastnes doe hate
> And changed be: yet being rightly wayd
> They are not changed from their first estate;
> But by their change their being doe dilate:
> And turning to themselves at length againe,
> Do worke their owne perfection so by fate:

> Then ouer them Change doth not rule and raigne;
> But they raigne ouer change, and do their states maintaine.
>
> (Spenser 1978: *Mut.* 7.58)

This turn back to an everlasting essence suggests that the dilation and deferral of romance are simply momentary lapses. Yet the tellingly "vnperfite" last canto recognizes Mutabilitie's "greatest sway" on this earth. The eternal rest of the Heavens is not of this world, but belongs to an apocalyptic endpoint of time. Despite the poet's longing for rest, the final lines recognize the distance between his condition, bound by earth and change, and the stasis that will only come with the relinquishment of earthly things. As Ariosto recognized, the deferral of romance, incomplete and unsatisfying though it might seem, postpones the inevitability of death.

CHIVALRY AND ITS SEQUELS

The early modern development of printing exacerbated the striking iterability of romance already evident in the medieval manuscript tradition. The printing press enabled the wide circulation of new texts but also gave new life to older stories, disseminating them to a broader audience (Goodman 1998: 28). While the sixteenth century saw a new vogue for pastoral and Greek romance, the appeal of chivalric romance was unsurpassed. As Jennifer Goodman suggests, even the division between "medieval" and "renaissance" is highly debatable for chivalric romance, which experienced an uninterrupted popularity across Europe from the earliest Chrétien narratives until well into the seventeenth century.

By the sixteenth century, chivalric romance in prose, in particular, had become endlessly generative: the feats of one hero continued in a new volume on the achievements of his son, seemingly ad infinitum. In Spain the phenomenon has received particular attention, due to Cervantes' brilliant parody of the genre in *Don Quijote* (1605, 1615). Cervantes points to Garci Rodríguez de Montalvo's *Amadís of Gaul* (1508), itself a revision and continuation of a lost fourteenth-century text, as "the first chivalric romance printed in Spain," and origin of all the rest (Cervantes 1995: I.6). Although its precise textual history is unclear, there is no question that the story of the wandering prince, exposed as a child and unaware of his own identity, his love for the princess Oriana, and his protection by the enchantress Urganda the Unknown, inaugurates a virtual craze for the romances of chivalry.

Amadís was itself reprinted fifteen times over the course of the sixteenth century, while the adventures of his son, *Las sergas de Esplandián*, and grandson, *Lisuarte de Grecia*, each went through multiple editions. The chivalric sagas of the first age of print seem strikingly modern in this respect, profiting from their immense popularity by reproducing themselves in sequels, imitations, and so forth, yet medieval romance, too, often proliferated in this fashion, although largely within the confines of manuscript culture. One might argue that here lie the origins of one of our more belittling contemporary associations with romance, as "genre literature," endlessly iterated to fulfill the insatiable demands of readers. Harry Sieber provides a useful account of this textual generation:

> Multiplication of plots within plots introduces more characters, more examples of love and valor, and, as we have seen, more description. But in the end the characters, stories, and examples are much the same; only their names, locations, and associates change. Amplification and repetition relate one romance to another in structural and thematic terms, variety helps to sustain their illusion of uniqueness.
>
> (Sieber 1985: 212)

Thus the romances of chivalry become longer and more complex, without necessarily achieving any greater sophistication. As Sieber suggests, the reader can easily see through the limited variations, but does not necessarily find this a failing. Chivalric romance becomes, in a sense, the first mass genre, purveying quantities of prose to a literate but relatively uneducated audience in search of comforting familiarity. A central set of topoi are endlessly repeated: a historically and often geographically remote setting, the mysterious origins of the hero, separation and reunion, disguise and recognition, magic and enchantments. Yet despite their marked artificiality, the romances of chivalry often exhibit what Daniel Eisenberg calls "pseudo-historicity," presenting themselves as historical texts more akin to chronicle than to fable (Eisenberg 1982: 127–8). This attempt at legitimization is reminiscent of Chrétien's efforts to validate the early *roman* by granting it an ancient textual source, as in the famous prologue to *Cligés*, discussed in Chapter 2. Later chivalric romances often claim authority by alluding to a textual tradition comprising one or more historians whose versions of events must be evaluated and reconciled by the narrator (Eisenberg 1982: 127). Despite the fictional nature of these sources, the narratives thus obliquely acknowledge romance's embeddedness in a textual tradition that rehearses, amplifies, and revisits earlier material, presenting other versions or segments of the story.

Despite (or perhaps because of) their rote repetition and predictability, chivalric romances became inordinately popular. They are explicitly referred to by such unexpected readers as the Carmelite nun and reformer Saint Teresa of Avila, who notes in her autobiography (c. 1565) how, despite the *paterfamilias'* objections, her mother and her siblings shared her fascination with the books:

> [My mother] was fond of books of chivalry; and this pastime had not the ill effects on her that it had on me, because she never allowed them to interfere with her work. But we were always trying to make time to read them; and she permitted this, perhaps in order to stop herself from thinking of the great trials she suffered, and to keep her children occupied so that in other respects they should not go astray. This annoyed my father so much that we had to be careful lest he should see us reading these books. For myself, I began to make a habit of it, and this little fault which I saw in my mother began to cool my good desires and lead me to other kinds of wrongdoing. I thought there was nothing wrong in my wasting many hours, by day and by night, in this useless occupation, even though I had to hide it from my father. So excessively was I absorbed in it that I believe, unless I had a new book, I was never happy.
>
> (Teresa 1991: 68–9)

Saint Teresa underscores both the moral dangers of the romances, in that they lead to other kinds of wrongdoing, and the pleasure they provide. Women and children, she suggests, are especially vulnerable to the seduction of these books, whose pleasures must be hidden from the patriarchal authority.

The romances are singled out as a noxious influence on impressionable readers, particularly young women, by humanist moralists such as Juan

Luis Vives. In his 1528 manual, *The Education of a Christian Woman*, he describes them as "books filled with endless absurdities":

> I wonder what it is that delights us in these books unless it be that we are attracted by indecency. Learning is not to be expected from authors who never saw even a shadow of learning. As for their storytelling, what pleasure is to be derived from the things they invent, full of lies and stupidity? One hero killed twenty singled-handed, another slew thirty, and still another hero left for dead with six hundred gaping wounds suddenly rises to his feet and the next day, restored to health and strength, lays two giants low in a single battle, then proceeds on his way, laden with gold, silver, silks, and jewels in such quantity that even a cargo ship could not carry them.
>
> (Vives 2000: 75–6)

Vives is particularly exercised by the appeal of texts that provide nothing but pleasure, with no redeeming moral, exemplary, or educational value. He also denounces the romances' imaginative force, and in particular their reliance on the marvelous, as though their very departure from verisimilitude made them pernicious. Renaissance writers and literary theorists struggled with precisely these questions: To what extent could a writer stretch verisimilitude, or abandon it altogether, for the sake of readerly pleasure? Did the use of the marvelous preclude all moral value for a text? The attempt to reconcile readerly pleasure, or what we might call reception, with prescriptive categories for literary creation was one of the central strands in sixteenth-century theoretical debates.

ROMANCE IN THE NEW WORLD

Strikingly, the material excess that Vives condemns as unrealistic: "gold, silver, silks, and jewels in such quantity that even a cargo ship could not carry them" – recalls an actual historical referent, the Spanish conquest of the Aztec empire, which occurred only a few years before Vives' manual was written. In the New World, Spanish conquerors resorted to chivalric romance as they searched for a way to describe the marvelous sights that they encountered. Most famously, the aging soldier Bernal Díaz del Castillo, who wrote his *History of the Conquest of New Spain* (1568) almost fifty years after the fact, described Mexico via an explicit reference to *Amadís*:

> Next morning, we came to a broad causeway and continued our march toward Iztapalapa. And when we saw all those cities and villages built in the water, and other great towns on dry land, and that straight and level causeway leading to Mexico, we were astounded. These great towns and *cues* [temples] and buildings rising from the water, all made of stone, seemed like an enchanted vision from the tale of Amadís. Indeed, some of our soldiers asked whether it was not all a dream. It is not surprising therefore that I should write in this vein. It was all so wonderful that I do not know how to describe this first glimpse of things never heard of, seen or dreamed of before.
>
> (Díaz del Castillo 1963: 214)

While Bernal Díaz recognizes that his comparison is metaphorical, other explorers sought in the marvelous New World actual instantiations of the romance world. Thus, for example, certain early contracts of exploration included specific instructions to search for the Amazons, figures newly popularized by the *Amadís* sequel *Las sergas de Esplandián* (Leonard 1992: 36). *Las sergas* also gives us the name California, the island that was home to the Amazon queen in that romance (Vogeley 2001). Romance thus exhibits very real historical effects: it both provides the impetus for exploration and leaves its mark on the landscape.

Beyond its description of marvelous places and beings, chivalric romance speaks to the enterprise of conquest through its "geographical impulse," evident in Ariosto's winged hippogryph (Parker 1990: 611), and its accounts of successful encounters with the Other, as well as its glorification of the quest. Romance provides a vocabulary for describing travel and travelers in sympathetic, even heroic terms (Goodman 1998: 56). More specifically, Michael Nerlich notes how early capitalism connects mercantile and colonial enterprises to chivalry through the richly polysemic term *adventure* (Nerlich 1987: 52 and passim). Thus by the sixteenth century, the adventure of discovery could be glorified as both a heroic and a mercantile pursuit. Note how the language of romance pervades this 1553 speech by a royal representative in praise of a new English merchant company:

> [The adventurer] commits his life (a thing to a man of all things more
> deare) to the raging Sea, and the uncertainties of many dangers . . . We
> shall keepe our owne coastes and countrey: Hee shall seeke strange and
> unknowen kingdomes. He shall commit his safetie to barbarous
> and cruell people, and shall hazard his life amongst the monstrous and
> terrible beastes of the sea.
>
> (cited in Nerlich 1987: 129)

Here is the explorer as a new Odysseus, a second Amadís. The construction
of essentially mercantile activity as an ennobling pursuit reaches its logical
conclusion in Elizabeth's glorification of privateers, who were often lowly
subjects like Martin Frobisher and Francis Drake, knighted for their
successful plunder of Spanish ships and coasts. (The crown's active role
in transforming piracy into a chivalric enterprise is but another way in
which Elizabeth harnesses the language of courtly chivalry to strengthen
her position as a female ruler, as I discussed earlier.) The culmination of
this process lies in the full-fledged fictional "romance of empire" that
accompanies British expansion at its nineteenth-century peak.

Although it might seem ideally suited to the enterprise of empire, it is
also possible to read romance as the deflation of epic purpose and imperial
conquest. Romance may offer a respite from the battlefield or an alternative
way to imagine the relations between peoples. One striking example of
this dynamic, in both formal and thematic terms, is Alonso de Ercilla's
La Araucana (1569–97), an epic on the uprising of the Araucanians
(Mapuches) against the Spanish conquistadors in Chile. The narrator is
Ercilla himself, who witnesses most of the battles first-hand. Yet the strain
of this proximity makes him oddly reluctant to continue with his story of
blood and gore, and he longs for a reprieve. This is conveniently (and
ironically) provided by none other than Reason personified, who breaks
off a prophecy about Spain's future to grant the narrator his romance
interlude:

> But if Mars' furor and ferocity
> Have distempered your pen
> And you would mix with its harshness
> Soft and easeful matter,
> Turn your eyes, see the beauty

> Of Spain's ladies, for I know not
> How, given the good contained there,
> Love does not consume the world.
>   (Ercilla 1993: 18.64, my translation)

The poet is immediately granted a vision of "paradise": a fertile, green meadow complete with running stream and beautiful ladies (Ercilla 1993: 18.66–7). But as he is about to launch into his "amorous song," a welcome respite from "rough bloody wars" (Ercilla 1993: 18.72), he wakes to shouts of battle. In Ercilla, interlace becomes a technique for coping with unspeakable violence. Over and over again, the poet truncates his text "in order to defeat narrative incorporation of a violence that exceeds explanatory or ideological structure" (Quint 1993: 164).

Romance also provides an important conduit for sympathy. Several episodes focus on the Araucanian women and their fierce love for their men. A particularly striking instance casts the unfortunate Glaura as a damsel in distress, suffering through the ravages of war and constant assaults on her virginity (Ercilla 1993: 28). The story culminates with the revelation that her lost husband and protector, Cariolán, is none other than the *yanacona*, or captive Indian, whom Ercilla has saved from death at hands of the Spaniards, and who returns the favor by warning him of an Indian ambush. The negotiation of power and commiseration here is complex: the price of romance empathy seems to be the taming of Cariolán, "domesticated, where he had once been indomitable" (Ercilla 1993: 28.52). Yet in the heat of the new battle Ercilla unceremoniously grants both Cariolán and Glaura their freedom, commending them to God, itself a peculiar resolution when the struggle against the Araucanians is far from over.

Despite its overall epic form, *La Araucana*'s resolution is undone by romance. Ercilla's narrative wanders far and wide, in marvelous scenes of prophecy complete with crystal ball and native soothsayer. Yet while the "geographical impulse" often serves to chart Spain's greatness as a universal empire, it takes the narrator away from the pressing problems of the Chilean revolt that he relates as a contemporary event. And the uncertainty of Spain's position in Chile is never resolved: the narrator leaves the Araucanians in the midst of their war council, "filled with new rage and greater ire" (Ercilla 1993: 34.35), determined to choose a new leader and continue their resistance. Then, in a complex sequence of interlace, Ercilla takes us on a marvelous expedition into southern Chile, an odd mixture of pastoral enchantment and hazardous voyage, and relates his subsequent experiences in the New World (Ercilla 1993: 35, 36). Eventually, he berates himself for having abandoned his story of Arauco (Ercilla 1993: 36.42), and promises to continue. But as soon as he has finished clearing his throat, so to speak, he again leaves Chile behind to relate Philip II's conquest of Portugal, which is a more straightforward, and definitive, victory (Ercilla 1993: 36.44 and following). The entire last canto is devoted to this Portuguese material, and thus the story of Arauco remains inconclusive and unresolved, as the narrator replaces epic finality with open-endedness. Both formally and thematically, then, romance complicates the verities of imperial epic, foregrounding sympathy, wandering, and inconclusiveness over the finality of conquest.

MAD FOR CHIVALRY

With Miguel de Cervantes' *Don Quijote* (1605, 1615), the deflation of romance becomes as notable and important a literary strategy as romance itself. Almost immediately reprised in the English comedy by Francis Beaumont *The Knight of the Burning Pestle* (1607), and quickly translated into a variety of languages, *Don Quijote* addresses many of the controversies over romance in its pages, even as it evinces its enduring popularity. In the first age of print, the difference between the world of books, particularly chivalric romance, and a real world of war, scarcity, and madness yields some of Cervantes' most inspired satirical scenes. Don Quijote deliberately follows the conventions of romance to construct himself as a knight: he chooses an idealized beloved, Dulcinea of Toboso (actually the swineherd Aldonza Lorenzo), has himself dubbed knight (by a lowly innkeeper), and sets off to fight giants (which look remarkably like windmills to everyone else). The fond satire allows us to reconstruct the hallmarks of chivalric romance and also its immense popularity. In *Don Quijote*, the romance marvelous that so vexed Tasso is nicely contained in the protagonist's imagination. Don Quijote is the besotted romance reader *par excellence*, so convinced of the paramount truth of the books that he constantly struggles to fit reality within their parameters. When the world around him diverges, and the windmills resolutely remain windmills, he ascribes the difference to malevolent enchanters, thereby reinscribing his reality into the world of the texts (Foucault 1973: 47). Don Quijote's isolation in his madness ironizes the solitary knight's quest. Once he finds a companion in the squire Sancho Panza, however, their exchanges provide a dialogic perspective on their condition, with the squire challenging the would-be knight's constant idealization of what surrounds him.

Although he parodies the besotted readers of romance, Cervantes also pokes fun at their critics, in a series of episodes that read like a *summa* of sixteenth-century literary debates. In the early mock-Inquisition of Don Quijote's library, the barber and the priest, self-appointed guardians of Don Quijote, burn most of his romances of chivalry, though they make pointed exceptions for, among others, *Amadís* and the Catalan Arthurian romance *Tirant lo Blanc* (Cervantes 1995: I.6). The credulity of Don Quijote's housekeeper, who advocates the burning yet worries that the books' enchanters may take revenge, easily matches his own. Elsewhere, Cervantes underscores the wide appeal of the books, as the Innkeeper describes the communal enjoyment of romances, read aloud at harvest time for an audience of delighted laborers (Cervantes 1995: I.32). Regardless of its debatable historical accuracy, this episode suggests Cervantes' appreciation of the pleasure that the romances provide.

A more explicit discussion of the chivalric romances' literary value takes place between the priest and the Canon of Toledo, at the end of Part I. The Canon trots out all the familiar objections to the books: their indistinctness, the empty pleasure they provide, their lack of verisimilitude or of unity:

> Truly, your reverence, I myself hold these so-called books of chivalry to be a danger to our country, and though I have read at least the first pages of almost all that have been published, impelled by an idle and treacherous whim, I've never been able to read a single one from beginning to end, for they seem to me – some more, some less – pretty much all of a piece, one just like the other, and there's nothing more to this one than that one. So this sort of writing seems to me to belong to the genre of tales and fables they call Milesian, which are wildly nonsensical stories seeking only to give pleasure, and not to teach anything – exactly the opposite of moral fables, which both delight and teach at the same time. And since the chief purpose of such books is to

give pleasure, I don't understand how they can possibly do that, filled as they are with so much wild nonsense . . . For what beauty, what harmony of one part with the whole, and the whole with all its parts, can there be in a book or a tale in which a sixteen year old boy can cut a giant as tall as a tower right in half, with one blow, and as easily as if the giant were made of sugar paste? . . . And to anyone who answers by saying that people who write such books are creating fictions [*cosas de mentira*, lying things] and therefore aren't obliged to worry about fine points or truth, I say to them that the best lies are those that most closely resemble truth, and what gives the most pleasure is what seems most probable or possible . . . I've yet to see a single book of chivalry which truly holds together, with the middle matching the beginning, and the end corresponding to both the beginning and the middle; instead they're composed in so many scattered pieces that they seem to be meant as puzzles or monstrosities rather than balanced entities.

(Cervantes 1995: I.47)

Despite his protestations, the Canon is clearly an avid reader of romances, intimately familiar with their failings, from beginning to end. In fact, as he then confesses, he has even attempted to write one himself, although he abandons the attempt when he realizes, by examining the contemporary stage, that popular taste is not guided by Aristotelian prescriptions (Cervantes 1995: I.48). Through this implicit comparison to the enormously successful *comedias* of the Spanish playwright Lope de Vega (1562–1635), themselves often full of romance motifs, Cervantes underscores the romances' efficacy in transcending the parameters of sixteenth-century theory.

In fact, Don Quijote himself launches into an impassioned defense of the romances. He begins by claiming the truth of a romance heroism that is indistinguishable from historical feats: "all the many, many glorious deeds performed by Christian knights from this and other countries, every one of them authenticated and truthful" (Cervantes 1995: I.49), and thus reminds us of the essential connections between chivalric romance and fanciful national historiographies. He soon moves, however, to a passionate defense of readerly pleasure, creating his own archetypal romance for his listener's delectation:

> Could there be anything more satisfying than to see, as it were, right in front of our eyes, an immense lake of bubbling, boiling pitch, crawling with hordes of wriggling serpents, and snakes, and lizards, and all sorts of fierce and terrifying animals – and then, right out of the middle of that lake, there comes a doleful voice, saying: "You, knight, whoever you may be, staring out at this fearful lake, if you yearn for the treasure hidden under these black waters, show the strength of your brave heart and hurl yourself into the middle of this black and burning tide . . ."

The valorous knight of course dives right in, only to find below the waters the pastoral and erotic plenitude with which romance rewards courage:

> The sky in that place shines clearer, and the sun glows with a new brightness, and the knight sees spread out in front of him a peaceful forest, trees so luxuriantly green that just seeing them is sheer delight. Here there's a small stream, whose cool fresh waters flow like liquid crystal over the fine sand and polished white stones, looking for all the world like powdered gold and the purest of pearls, and there is a fountain beautifully crafted in multi-colored jasper and smooth marble, and over there yet another fountain, more crudely fashioned, on which are clustered tiny mussel shells and the spiralled white and yellow dwellings that snails carry on their backs, all set so wildly and profusely, and so intermixed with bits of gleaming crystal and imitation emeralds that it forms a shape of such wild elaboration that art, in the process of imitating nature, seems to have overwhelmed it . . . And after seeing all this, what could be better than to find a crowd of lovely maidens coming through the gates? so charmingly and beautifully dressed that, were I now to describe them as they are described in these books, there would be no end to what I might say.
>
> (Cervantes 1995: I.50)

Don Quijote is hardly a suspicious reader. Engrossed in his own pleasure, and fully identifying with the rewarded knight, he fails to recognize this landscape with maidens as the threatening Bower of Bliss that so exercises Tasso and Spenser. Instead he relishes the relentless idealization of romance. Despite, or perhaps because of, those faults emphasized by Vives and other humanist moralists, such as exaggeration, lack of verisimilitude, and sensuality, Don Quijote's romance provides him with great satisfaction. His creation is also a rebuke of sorts to the severe strictures of classicism: the two unmatched fountains, whose "wild elaboration" goes beyond respectful imitation to "overwhelm" nature suggest a different set of aesthetic parameters altogether. Assessing romance according to Aristotelian rules will therefore never yield a full appreciation; only the proper consideration of variety, inspiring idealization, and readerly pleasure will ensure that the romances receive their due.

Don Quijote's own failed adventures constantly undercut his claims for the viability, and essential reality, of the romances. The fantasy of his romance creation is immediately undercut when he claims that, although he is currently "shut up in a crate like a madman," he expects his valor will soon result in his becoming an emperor, with sufficient riches to "exhibit the graciousness and generosity held here in my heart" (Cervantes 1995: I.50). The material and the real continuously trump the idealization of romance, despite Don Quijote's conscious attempt to distance himself from the everyday. When the would-be knight claims that he cannot pay the innkeeper because he does not carry money, for example, his host quickly points out the limitations of the romance world-view: "The innkeeper told him that on this matter he was quite mistaken, because although it was true that the stories omitted such details – for it seemed to their authors unnecessary to write about plain and essential subjects like money and clean shirts – this was no reason to think knight errants didn't need money" (Cervantes 1995: I.3). The innkeeper also mocks chivalric adventure by comparing it to his own picaresque wanderings, structurally analogous if very different in their material concerns and unflinching realism:

> He told Don Quijote that he himself, in his youth, had given himself up to the same honorable profession, travelling to different parts of the world, seeking adventures, including such notable spots as the Fish Market at Málaga, the Laughing Islands, the Crossroads in Seville, the Marketplace in Segovia, the Olive Warehouse in Valencia, the Bandstand in Granada, the beach at San Lúcar, the horsetrack in Córdoba, the bars in Toledo, and all kinds of other places, where he'd had lots of practice being light on his feet, quick with his hands, perpetrating injustice, wooing widows, seducing virgins, cheating schoolboys and,

> to make a long story short, making a name for himself in who knows
> how many courts and tribunals virtually everywhere in all of Spain.
>
> (Cervantes 1995: I.3)

The picaresque landscape limned by the innkeeper challenges the idealized geographies of romance, replacing valor with guile and knightly deeds with petty crime, and problematizing the way romance imagines heroism in terms of the individual. Such passages represent a new literary mode, anticipated by Ariosto: the tension between romance and realism, between idealization and the mundane everyday.

A key instance of this struggle in the text is Don Quijote's stubborn insistence that an ordinary barber's bowl is the enchanted golden helmet of Mambrino, from Boiardo and Ariosto (Cervantes 1995: I.25). Don Quijote tellingly picks up on the almost fetishistic value of objects in chivalric romance: magic rings, armor, and so forth, but chooses a laughable example. While Don Quijote insists on the authenticity of his trophy, for this is one of his few successful adventures, Sancho compromises, deeming the receptacle a *baciyelmo*, or basin-helmet (Cervantes 1995: I.45). The compromise marks the perspectivism of the text (Spitzer 1948: 59–60), and its constant negotiation between the textual authority of the romance precedents and the hard reality of Don Quijote's world.

For if Don Quijote is an uncritical reader of Ariosto, Cervantes reads him very carefully: like his predecessor, he points out both the anachronism of chivalric ideology and its contradictions, and plays constantly with narrative authority. The romance motif of pseudo-historicity is parodied in the narrator's claim to have found the second (and longest) part of *Don Quijote* among scrap papers for sale in the Toledo market. The Arabic manuscript, by a certain Cide Hamete Benengeli, was translated by a disenfranchised *morisco*, a Moor forcibly converted to Christianity, in exchange for two bushels of raisins. This lowly textual transaction replaces the *translatio studii* of Chrétien's prologue, or Ariosto's constant dialogue with his classical models. The Benengeli pre-text suggests how even the most clichéd motifs of romance may be imbued with ideological force and political currency: for Cervantes to ascribe his text to a disenfranchised people, and to claim an original in a proscribed language, is a forceful gesture of inclusiveness and tolerance. *Don Quijote* claims an original, and a textual transmission not in the classical languages of Greece or Rome, or in the triumphant European vernaculars that emulate their authority, but in the language of the defeated Moors, those habitual romance enemies who in this case, paradoxically, produce and disseminate the text.

Beyond the parody of textual origins, Cervantes carefully distances his protagonist from the marvelous heroics of the *Furioso*:

> As a mere hidalgo, a nobleman of the lowest possible rank, Don Quijote lacks social and economic position. His separation from the aristocratic and courtly world is foregrounded by geography. While Ariosto's knights travel the world and even go to the moon, Don Quijote searches for adventure in the dry and prosaic plains of La Mancha. His one celestial voyage is a hoax, and Clavileño a purposely wooden imitation of Ariosto's hippogryph.
>
> (De Armas 2002: 43)

In a sense, *Don Quijote* chronicles the marginalization of chivalry, from military action to courtly conduct (Cascardi 2002: 70). By Part II, an increasingly disillusioned Don Quijote mourns the loss of true chivalry:

> Our depraved age does not deserve that blessing, as former ages did, when knights errant shouldered and took on themselves the defense of kings, the protection of damsels, the succoring of orphans and wards of court, the punishment of the proud, and the rewarding of the humble. With most of our knights, today, it's the damasks, brocades, and other rich fabrics they wear that rustle as they go, rather than any coats of armor; knights no longer sleep out in the fields, open to all the rigors of the heavens, lying there, armed and armored head to foot; no longer do they try to snatch forty winks, as it's called, without pulling their feet out of the stirrups, but only leaning on their lances, as the knights of old used to do. No longer do they sweep out of a wood, here, and up a mountain, there, and then tramp along a barren, deserted seashore, usually in stormy, angry weather, and then find themselves, right at the water's edge, a tiny boat without oars or a sail or a mast or any rigging or tackle whatever, but with intrepid hearts launch themselves out onto the waves, abandoning themselves to the implacable waves that break across the bottomless sea, on which, one moment, they are borne up toward the sky, and, the next, are pulled deep into the abyss; and setting

their breasts against the invincible tempest, find – though they could never have expected it – they're suddenly twenty thousand miles and more from where they set sail, and leaping out onto that distant, unknown land, they experience things worthy of being recorded not simply on paper or parchment, but on bronze. But today sloth triumphs over exertion, laziness over labor, vice over virtue, arrogance over bravery, and the theory of combat over its practice, which lived and shone only in the Age of Gold, the Age of Knight Errantry.

(Cervantes 1995: II.1)

The would-be knight's elegiac invocation of chivalry idealizes even his literary predecessors, who are rarely as uncomplicatedly virtuous as he would have them appear.

While Don Quijote yearns for the chivalric Age of Gold, Cervantes' ironic stance towards heroism rebukes Spain's own investment in imperial mythologies. If, in an earlier age, chivalric fiction had served to animate New World conquests, Cervantes' parodic rehearsal now pointedly critiques imperial delusions and the glorification of a martial ideal. This criticism targets not only Spanish expansionism abroad, but the so-called "Reconquista" of Islamic Al-Andalus. This protracted struggle against Islam on the Iberian Peninsula, culminating in the fall of Granada in 1492, was enshrined in the sixteenth century as the centerpiece of Spanish heroism and Spain's glory. In this vision, the Reconquista knight was motivated by religious devotion and the goal of a Christian, unified Spain. By contrast, Don Quijote's own more interested desires for political power, such as his quest to become an emperor and endow Sancho with his own island fiefdom, paint a very different picture of chivalry than the ideal of the selfless knight. As critics have argued in recent years, Cervantes' critique of chivalric romance here expands into a broad indictment of Spain's imperial expansion (Wilson 2000, 2002).

Beyond *Don Quijote*, Cervantes uses the conventions of romance in a highly deliberate fashion. His *Exemplary Novels* (1613) provide some of the most interesting examples of romance as strategy. In these short narratives, Cervantes plays with the conventionality and idealization of romance, using them as a convenient screen for political and ideological critiques. While critics have largely preferred the "realist" novellas, it is in the "idealist" ones that this dynamic comes through most clearly. As recent criticism has shown, texts such as "The English-Spanish Girl," concerned with the enmity between Spain and England, and "The Generous Lover," a captivity narrative set in the Eastern Mediterranean, are fully engaged with their historical context (Johnson 2001, Fuchs 2003), although the force of that engagement is often disguised by the trappings of romance: relentless idealization of the protagonists, coincidences, separations and marvelous reappearances, and so forth. Thus the hero of "The English-Spanish Girl," forced by Elizabeth I to become a privateer in order to win his lady, agonizes about his relative allegiance to Catholicism and to England, a dilemma marvelously resolved when he encounters Turkish rather than Spanish ships. In "The Generous Lover," meanwhile, the escaped captives exhibit a blithe fascination for all things Turkish, which they bring back with them to Sicily. Once there, as they are paired off in a happy romance ending, the renegades among them are also unproblematically incorporated into the Christian community. Thus the expected and comforting moves of romance serve Cervantes to challenge such ideological behemoths as the role of religious difference in national identity, or the exclusionary nature of Spain's Catholicism. Romance may pose its own explicit challenge to these ideologies, as in the many instances of individual knights who cross religious and national lines with impunity. Or it may simply present a pointed, striking contrast to the historical context in which its idealizing fictions are being invoked.

LITERARY HIERARCHIES AND THE SHAKESPEAREAN FALLACY

Early modern England has a rich tradition of romance in both verse and prose. Some of these texts exist at the very center of the canon: Spenser's *Faerie Queene*, the highly regarded but less often read *Arcadia* (c. 1580) by Sir Philip Sidney. Others have been relatively neglected: Mary Wroth's *Urania* (1621) for example, has only recently been recovered by feminist critics. There is also a broad corpus of popular prose romance: versions of continental medieval favorites and newer chivalric, pastoral or Greek romances, as well as reworkings of homegrown romances from centuries past. Yet despite this varied and well-documented tradition, the most common use of the term romance in the field refers to a subset of Shakespeare's late plays. This peculiar typology has the unfortunate consequence of obscuring the many genres with a claim to being considered English Renaissance romances, all of which are typically neglected for the highly anomalous category of dramatic romance. It also reinforces the Bard's exceptionalism, cutting off his production from that of his contemporaries.

Shakespeare's contemporaries, or indeed the dramatist himself, never used the term as a generic classification; it is an entirely retrospective and anachronistic designation. The romancing of Shakespeare begins with Samuel Taylor Coleridge's 1808 description of the plays as "a different genus, diverse in kind, not merely different in degree, – romantic dramas, or dramatic romances." But Coleridge's definition is in no way historical; he is not attempting to equate Shakespeare with Greek or Renaissance romances, but rather with "the true genuine modern poetry," the *romantic*. The analogy is singularly obscure, resting as it does on Coleridge's judgment that both are, "more rich, more expressive and various, as one formed out of a chaos by more obscure affinities of atoms apparently heterogeneous" (Coleridge 1959: 51). In his *Notes on The Tempest*, ten years later, Coleridge stresses romantic drama's removal from history and reality:

> *The Tempest*, I repeat, has been selected as a specimen of the romantic drama; that is, of a drama, the interests of which are independent of all historical facts and associations, and arise from their fitness to that faculty of our nature, the imagination I mean, which owes no allegiance to time and place, – a species of drama, therefore, in which errors in chronology and geography, no mortal sins in any species, are venial, or count for nothing.
>
> (Coleridge 1959: 203)

Coleridge's insistence on the ahistoricism of no less than *The Tempest*, a text that has recently been contextualized by reference to the discourse of colonialism in the Americas, in Ireland and in the Mediterranean, underscores how much historical debris can be swept under the magic carpet of romance illusionism. It is important to note, however, that, unlike later critics, Coleridge does not establish romance as a subcategory of Shakespearean drama; instead, he brings all of Shakespeare up to date, as it were, by conferring on it the honorific title of *romantic*. This inclusion of the illustrious ancestor from Stratford in the romantic club not only serves to legitimate the new but contributes to the exceptionalism of the

old, making Shakespeare presumably more readable in the context of
the early nineteenth century than in his own time: as Coleridge himself put
it, "Shakespeare is of no age" (Coleridge 1959: 107). Thus, although this
first "romantic" critic did not propose romance as an internal classification
for Shakespearean drama, he did establish the connection between the
term, an ahistorical reading of the texts, and the exceptionalism of their
author. Romance literally makes Shakespeare *sui generis*. These are the
connections that later criticism, more fully taxonomic, would develop into
a proper category of Shakespearean romance.

In the First Folio (1623), the plays we have become accustomed to
thinking of as romances were summarily classified as either comedy, as in
the case of *A Winter's Tale* and *The Tempest*, or tragedy, as in the case of
Cymbeline. These three plays, along with *Pericles*, were first singled out
as members of a special class by Edward Dowden in his 1879 study of
Shakespeare, where he argues that in them,

> We suddenly pass to beauty and serenity; from the plays concerned with
> the violent breaking of human bonds, to a group of plays which are all
> concerned with the knitting together of human bonds, the reunion of
> parted kindred, the forgiveness of enemies, the atonement for wrong
> . . . The dramas have a grave beauty, a sweet serenity, which seem to
> render the name "comedies" inappropriate; we may smile tenderly, but
> we never laugh loudly, as we read them. Let us, then, name this group,
> consisting of four plays, Romances.
>
> (Dowden 1879: 54–6)

For Dowden, the category of romance completes the "true order of
succession" of the plays, culminating in *The Tempest*, "Shakespeare's
highest and serenest view of life" (Dowden 1879: 150). This ostensible
progression reinforces the connection between romance as a category and
humanist readings that emphasize magic and mystical scenes of restitution
and reconciliation. Dowden's taxonomy replaces the generalized historicism
of Coleridge's "dramatic romance" with a literary history closely tied to
Shakespeare's biography:

> The writer of these exquisite plays, *Cymbeline*, *The Winter's Tale*, *The
> Tempest*, has none of the lightness of heart which is the property of

youth; he knows the wrongs of life; he sees the errors of men; but he seems to have found a resting-place of faith, hope, charity. The dissonances are resolved into a harmony; the spirit of the plays is one of large benignity; they tell of the blessedness of the forgiveness of injuries; they show how broken bonds between heart and heart may be repaired and reunited; each play closes with a victory of love.

(Dowden 1879: 82)

The generic mapping of the plays onto life thus imagines metaphorical trajectories for the drama without the need ever to interrogate the culture of the period. The plays become stagings of reconciliation late in life.

Dowden's own definition is unabashedly circular: the plays have romance elements; therefore they are romances. Later and more sophisticated accounts of the role of romance in Shakespeare attempt to escape the circularity by tethering their claims firmly in Greek Romance or in the continental romance tradition of Boccaccio and Ariosto (Gesner 1970, Pettet 1949). And indeed, *Pericles* is clearly based on the Apollonius story; *A Winter's Tale* on Robert Greene's romance *Pandosto*. But the studies of origins are, if anything, *too* successful, tracing the romance motifs in Shakespeare's plays so well that few of them can escape the category of romance. E.C. Pettet even goes so far as to suggest the broader category of "romantic comedies," and it is hard to argue with him. Voyages, shipwrecks, pirates, disguises, confusion, miraculous reunions are salient features of a play like *Twelfth Night*, which surely has its share of romance elements. But if the definition of Shakespearean romance is expanded to include this play and its like, the category becomes so large as to be meaningless. *Pace* Dowden, and as Lawrence Danson has noted, "the elements which compound one of [Shakespeare's] earliest plays, *The Comedy of Errors* – voyages over perilous seas to mysterious lands, the separation and eventual reunion of families, a sense of wonder approaching the realm of miracle – are the elements of *The Tempest* as well" (Danson 2000: 13). Danson wants to retain the category of Shakespearean romance, albeit advisedly. Yet the taxonomy depends on clear differences between categories, and once the plays begin to cross borders, the classification comes undone.

Shakespeare looms so large in early modern studies that it seems important to correct this strange, ahistorical categorization simply for the sake of Shakespeare studies. But there are larger considerations as well. The neglect of prose romance, occluded by the peculiar Shakespearean terminology, has for a long time distorted our sense of what was read in early modern England. As critics have recently pointed out, the "pleasant histories," as the popular prose romances were sometimes known, were the "core of popular literature" in the period (Newcomb 2002: 2, see also Spufford 1981), yet they have been relatively neglected by critics. This neglect uncritically reflects the hierarchies that have long organized this corpus, developed precisely in response to the newly diverse readership of the first age of print, which included more and more women and non-aristocratic readers. As Lori Newcomb has recently argued, the various versions of prose romance in the sixteenth century reveal much about how we derive categories of "high" and "low," elite and popular, literature (Newcomb 2002). Why do texts like Sidney's *Arcadia* and Robert Greene's *Pandosto* suffer such different critical fates, despite their similar reliance on pastoral and Greek romance models, and the tremendous popularity of the latter? Newcomb argues that it is precisely the popularity of *Pandosto* that classifies it as a part of a "subordinate cultural category" (Newcomb 2002: 1), read too widely to retain prestige. Literary value, at least where critics are concerned, thus appears to be inversely proportional to a text's breadth of readership.

Newcomb's project is crucial for interrogating the ways in which romance is increasingly marginalized as popular literature – a process that culminates with the "genre literature" of the nineteenth and twentieth centuries – and for challenging the purported emergence of the English novel, *ex nihilo*, in the eighteenth century. Moreover, as Newcomb points out, this kind of inquiry may help us broaden our concept of reading, and especially the reading of romances, so as to reflect the more generous parameters of cultural studies, "imagining pleasure reading as more than a cloak of false consciousness; seeking more diversified models for the cultural uses of reading, re-viewing the negotiation between low and high cultural forms as fully dynamic; resolving ambivalence about the materiality of print culture" (Newcomb 2002: 19). While these are all issues that I shall address at greater length in the next chapter, it is clear that the marginal-ization of romance as a lesser form begins at exactly the same point that it achieves its broad popularity via print circulation. The endless iterations of chivalric romance denounced by Vives while gently mocked by

Cervantes, and the English "pleasant histories" neglected by centuries of criticism are popular forms that literary history has paradoxically marginalized precisely because of their great success with readers, particularly those marked by their gender and class.

4

POST-RENAISSANCE
TRANSFORMATIONS

The trajectory of romance after the Renaissance is complex and often paradoxical. While Greek and chivalric romance, in particular, continued to prove hugely popular with readers, critical predilection for new kinds of narrative fiction led from an initial embrace of French "heroic" romance in the seventeenth century to the gradual marginalization of romance as a "low" genre in subsequent periods. In this final chapter, I trace the apotheosis and broad popularity of romance in its "heroic," "passionate," and "Gothic" incarnations, and the neoclassical condemnations of its excesses. Despite its vicissitudes, romance survived marked changes in literary fashion. As in the Renaissance, ancient romances continued to be published side by side with new fiction. Longus' *Daphnis and Chloe*, for example, was published more often in the eighteenth than in the sixteenth century (McMurran 2002: 55). In part, this popularity reflects how romance manages to adapt to the new fashion for "natural" or "orderly" narrative: some new editions of older romances abridge them, summarily rearrange them for the sake of clarity (Johnston 1964: 29–30), or even excise marvelous elements. Thus a helpful edition of *Ethiopica* from the early eighteenth century reorders the narrative to match the order in which the events had occurred (Kern 1968: 522). Romance also endures as children's literature: fantasies deemed appropriate for tender intellects, to be given over on reaching mature judgment (Johnston 1964: 27–30). Both as narrative strategy and in specific generic allusions, romance survives also in the very forms of fiction that are most often contrasted to romance: the "truthful" novella, or the realist novel. This ostensible opposition masks the frequent reliance of newer forms of realism on older romance structures. Finally, romance comes to animate a broad swath of popular literature and film, a development that both confirms its enduring appeal and seals its critical fate as a "low" form.

This chapter attempts to explain why, with some highly self-conscious exceptions, most critics no longer refer to narrative fiction as romance except to denigrate it. In the opposition between novel and romance, for example, the former is always the privileged term, and the latter slightly suspect. Yet despite recurrent efforts somehow to leave it behind, modernity continues to engage with romance, alternately embracing and rejecting it as a privileged mode of access to an idealized past, a vehicle for nostalgia, magic, and the imagination. Romance continues to be a powerful cultural force, even if its very strengths, such as its adaptability, iterability, and popularity, eventually banish it to the realm of "genre literature" and hence to mass paperbacks purchased in drugstores and supermarkets.

PASTORAL RETREAT, HEROIC EXCESS, PASSIONATE PLEASURE

There is no marked interruption in the fascination with various kinds of romance in sixteenth- and seventeenth-century France. Perhaps the best way to describe the transformation of romance in the latter period is by reference to its remarkable role within aristocratic culture. In the wake of translations of Longus and Heliodorus, the late sixteenth century sees a wave of French imitations of pastoral and Greek romances. In the seventeenth century these are developed into much longer narratives that attempt to convey a refined aesthetics of *bienséance* (decorum) and *vraisemblance* (verisimilitude), which is used to distinguish them from the perceived improbabilities of chivalric romance. Simultaneously, they reflect an ethical preoccupation with Neoplatonism and *préciosité*, the term used to describe the elaborate code of refinement developed in the aristocratic literary *salons* with which the romances are associated. Although the texts present the same framework as the Greek romances, and involve lovers separated by circumstance who must undergo endless perils and tribulations until they can finally achieve union, the characters' speech and behavior are often far more artificial and self-conscious than in the classical predecessors. At the same time, the texts become longer and more complex, with the typical romance running to several volumes and thousands of pages, its narrative continuously interrupted and lengthened by interpolated stories.

One central example of the "apotheosis" of romance in the early seventeenth century is Honoré d'Urfé's pastoral romance *Astrée*, published in five parts from 1607 to 1628. D'Urfé never finished it, leaving unachieved the deferred erotic consummation that animates so many hundreds of pages. Although *Astrée* is hardly an original text, revisiting the conventions of Jorge de Montemayor's *Diana*, Sidney's *Arcadia*, Cervantes' *Galatea*, and other sixteenth-century pastoral romances, and including other familiar genres in its interpolated narratives, it occupies a much more influential place within its culture. As critics have suggested, its vision of aristocrats who choose the life of shepherds, privileging virtue over wealth and repose over political influence creates a new, illusory sense of purpose for a disenfranchised aristocracy. Whereas Cervantes chooses to parody the irrelevance of the chivalric knight in the modern world, D'Urfé's romance, nearly contemporary with *Don Quijote*, constructs "for aristocratic readers a parochial and fictionalized historical vision of their chivalric feudal past by appropriating and modifying the conventions of romance" (Di Piero 1992: 49). In the words of another critic, "Loss of social and economic privilege is transmuted into a world-weary flight from the world" (Harth 1983: 47). As Erica Harth suggests, lack of political power is reconfigured as a gain in civility. And while wealth and influence are largely irrelevant in the pastoral world, orgins are not: a recognition scene revealing a noble birth always resolves the seeming flouting of hierarchy when two people of unequal status fall in love.

One of the concomitant features of this romance sublimation of powerlessness into refinement is the genre's increasing association with a feminine and feminized urban aristocratic culture. Some of the most important figures in literary salons at the time, both as authors and as patrons, were women, notably Madame de Rambouillet and Madame de

Scudéry. After D'Urfé, writers largely abandon the pastoral in favor of what is known as heroic or sentimental romance: Gomberville's *Polexandre* (1632); Scudéry's *Ibrahim* (1641), *Artamène* (1649), *Clélie* (1656), *Almahide* (1660); La Calprenède's *Cassandra* (1642), *Cléopatre* (1648), *Faramond* (1662). Although the setting changes from pastoral to Greek or "Oriental," the emphasis on the extreme idealization of the heroine, in particular, never wavers. Whether as shepherdess or as exotic queen, the heroine of these romances defends her virtue and observes the finer rules of etiquette, even when this requires, as in the case of Cleopatra, considerable rewriting of the historical record. But whereas this might make the romances less verisimilar, it reinforces their association with morality.

The most important French defender of romance, Bishop Pierre Daniel Huet, argues for its positive influence in his *On the Origins of Romance* (1670), translated into English in 1715. Huet argues that romance uses pleasure to make its moral teachings palatable, and does this so effectively that:

> Nothing so much refines and polishes Wit; Nothing conduces so much to the Forming and Advancing it to the Approbation of the World, as the Reading of Romances. These are the Dumb Tutors, which succeed those of the College, and teach us how to Live and Speak by a more Persuasive and Instructive Method than theirs, who deserve the Complement [sic] of *Horace* upon the *Iliad*, "That it teaches Morality more effectually, than the Precepts of the most Able Philosophers."
>
> (cited in Williams 1970: 54)

Not only is romance elevated to the level of epic, the practitioners of romance are elevated with it. Huet reveals and praises Scudéry's pseudonymous female authorship, casting her as "a Maid, as Illustrious in her Modesty, as her Merit" (cited in Williams 1970: 54).

Huet presents the contemporary heroic romance as a proximate, domestic model for French aristocratic morality, and is eager to claim French primacy, yet he also stresses the origins of romance in the East and in Africa: "'tis neither *Provence* nor *Spain*, as some are of Opinion, that we shall find to have given Birth to this agreeable Amusement: We must in the Pursuit of it, enquire into the remotest Countries, and derive our

Account from the most Latent Part of Antiquity" (cited in Williams 1970: 46, emphasis in original). As Doody points out, Huet here continues the work of Salmasius (Claude de Saumaise). In his 1640 edition of Achilles Tatius' Greek romance, *Leucippe and Clitophon*, Salmasius had emphasized the long history and cosmopolitanism of imaginative fiction, from the Persians to Asia Minor to the Arabs to the Spaniards and thence the French (Doody 1996: 258–61).

Despite its acknowledged exotic origins, even the historicity of the heroic romance is occasionally defended by its enthusiastic authors. Scudéry, for example, claims in the preface to her *Ibrahim*: "I have observed the manners, customes, Religions, and inclinations of people: And to give a more true resemblance to things, I have made the foundations of my work Historicall, my principal personages such as are marked out in the true History for illustrious persons, and the warres effective" (cited in Williams 1970: 4). Yet clearly what Scudéry calls "true resemblance" is not the same as what we could consider realism, but an idealized vision of "heroic" history carefully crafted to respect both moral and literary propriety.

The English translator's preface to *Artamène* (trans. 1691) makes a different claim for how heroic romance captures "the Truth of History":

> For the Intrigues and Miscarriages of War and Peace are better, many times, laid open and Satyriz'd in a *Romance*, than in a downright History, which being oblig'd to name the Persons, is often forc'd for several Reasons and Motives to be too partial and sparing; while such disguis'd Discourses as these, promiscuously personating every Man, and no Man, take their full liberty to speak the Truth.
>
> (cited in Williams 1970: 25)

In this version, romances simply have a different purchase on the truth: their very appearance of fantasy enables a more thorough critique of political agents. Yet clearly this truth, too, has little to do with empiricism; it connotes instead a moral stance towards political and historical events.

Critics of the heroic romance were quick to satirize its grand claims to historicity and moral superiority, emphasizing instead its artificiality and improbability. By the mid-seventeenth century, the reaction against romance produced a number of literary parodies: Scarron's *Roman Comique*, Molière's *Précieuses Ridicules*, and Furetière's *Le Roman Bourgeois*.

These poked fun at the conventions of the heroic romance, and exploited the often hilarious distance between an emerging middle class of readers and the improbable aristocratic characters that inspired them (McDermott 1989: 127).

While the heroic romance proved as popular in England as in France, in numerous translations as well as in texts written in English, by the turn of the eighteenth century the reaction against this literary fashion was sometimes couched in terms of national difference. The popular writer Delarivier Manley celebrated a new, shorter kind of fiction for her compatriots: "These little pieces which have banish'd Romances are much more agreeable to the Brisk and Impetuous Humour of the English, who have naturally no Taste for long-winded Performances, for they have no sooner begun a Book but they desire to see the End of it" (cited in Williams 1970: 33). The "little pieces" Manley described are variously referred to by modern critics as passionate romances or amatory novellas, in which, after many prurient near-escapes, the heroine's virtue is violently overcome by the predatory hero. In fact, these narratives represent neither a complete departure from French models nor a fundamental shift from the mechanics of romance narrative. John Richetti explains the popular amatory novella as "a simplification or vulgarization" rather than a substantive departure: "The great majority of the amorous novellas written in English before 1740 merely condensed the excesses of the heroic romance, substituted a debased and inflated but simplified heroic rant for the involved *préciosité* of the romances, and used that style to deliver stories of some external complication but of extreme moral and emotional simplicity" (Richetti 1969: 172–3). He notes the appeal of their "rich opportunities for pathetic and erotic involvement" for a broad audience unable to identify with the more exotic aspects of the heroic romances or to command the infinite leisure necessary to peruse them (173).

Richetti's account, although commendably interested in the popular-ization of narrative, nonetheless introduces both the hierarchies and chronologies typical of so much criticism on the novel: developments in fiction are measured as "healthy" (173) when they contribute to the "birth" of the novel in the 1740s; the contributions of popular narrative and of female authors, while acknowledged, are largely distinguished from serious fiction. Although more recent criticism, particularly by feminist scholars, has done much to dismantle these hierarchies, and brought new attention to bear on Manley, Eliza Haywood and other popular writers of sentimental fiction, the story of the birth of the novel has proved singularly resilient. In what follows, I will attempt to show how complicated it is to trace a clear separation between romance and novel, or a triumphant emergence of the latter that does not, in fact, rely heavily on the mechanics of the former.

ROMANCE VERSUS NOVEL

> I am afraid thy brains are a little disordered with Romances and Novels.
>
> Steele, *Spectator* 254, 1711

I focus here on English literature to assess the strange hierarchy introduced by juxtaposition of *novel* and *romance*, two terms used, at times interchangeably, for longer narrative fiction. As critics have observed, the very distinction does not exist in other European languages. For English literary history of the seventeenth and eighteenth centuries, however, the emergence of the novel, in its modern sense and as distinct from the shorter *novella*, and its separation from the romance are of central concern. More often than not, however, the distinction breaks down, with the terms used analogously, as in the quote above, or with critics' recognition that the traits considered exclusive to each kind of text actually appear in the other. The categories turn out to be remarkably flexible, to the point that part of what determines the characterization of a given text is its a priori valuation by critics. Thus an important aspect of romance as critical idiom in this period is its increasing marginalization as the less-favored category, associated with fantasy and the past instead of the realism increasingly valued by critical taste.

As I have noted above, in the late seventeenth and early eighteenth century, the fashion for French romances was in full swing in England. Although retrospectively the weakness for romances is attributed primarily to women, they were extremely popular with both male and female audiences, all consumed by the prevailing fashion. In Alexander Pope's satirical epic, *The Rape of the Lock* (1712), the young Baron "to *Love* an Altar built,/Of twelve vast *French* Romances, neatly gilt" (Pope 1940: II.37–8). Pope's satire targets not only the glorification and idealization of love ("neatly gilt") in the French romances but also their astounding girth: twelve of them might well provide a hundred volumes to use as construction materials.

The doubling of the terms for longer narrative fiction serves in part to claim a new beginning in England. This move, cannily identified by Doody, erases all those predecessors in realism, such as *Don Quijote*, the picaresque, domestic drama, recent French antecedents, as well as older narrative fiction, to claim eighteenth-century England as the birthplace of the novel and the locus of romance's long-overdue humbling. This strategy for promoting a national, modern production animated a series of extraordinarily rich exchanges in the burgeoning literary magazines of the period, and it continued to carry weight well into the twentieth century. *The Rise of the Novel*, Ian Watt's extraordinarily influential 1957 study, presents Daniel Defoe, Samuel Richardson, and Henry Fielding as the originators of a triumphant new literary form. Although he is far more interested in antecedents, Michael McKeon, in his *The Origins of the English Novel 1600–1740*, also concludes, somewhat paradoxically, with a "climax" of the origins in Richardson and Fielding (McKeon 1987: 410). As Richetti points out, "The history of the novel has thus been handed down to us as the triumph of an enlightened realism over reactionary romance, the development or evolution of a superior literary instrument" (Richetti 1969: 2). This history also erases the connections between earlier narrative fiction and the "new" writing, both of which, Richetti observes, participate in the emergence of "mass art," providing pleasurable identification for a broad audience (Richetti 1969: 5).

A survey of literary criticism from the period reveals that both authors and critics recognized the close similarities between romance and novel. In fact, for decades the terminology remained indistinct. Even though William Congreve, writing in 1691, already established a distinction between the "miraculous," "impossible" romance and the "familiar"novel (cited in Williams 1970: 27), the categories were still in flux in the middle of the eighteenth century. In fact, critics have argued that Congreve himself cannot be thinking of "novel" in the modern sense, but instead contrasts romance and *novella*. On the one hand, the OED cites several uses of *novel* for an extended narrative (distinct from a *novella*) long before the "new" writing of Richardson and Fielding. On the other hand, even at mid-century, Samuel Johnson, writing in the *Rambler*, still considers the popular fiction that others call the novel a type of romance:

The works of fiction with which the present generation seems more particularly delighted, are such as exhibit life in its true state, diversified only by accidents that daily happen in the world, and influenced by passions and qualities which are really to be found in conversing with mankind.

This kind of writing may be termed not improperly the comedy of romance, and is to be conducted nearly by the rules of comic poetry. Its province is to bring about natural events by easy means, and to keep up curiosity without the help of wonder; it is therefore precluded from the machines and expedients of the heroic romance, and can neither employ giants to snatch away a lady from the nuptial rites, nor knights to bring her back from captivity; it can neither bewilder its personages in deserts, nor lodge them in imaginary castles.

(cited in Williams 1970: 142–3)

Johnson values the new writing for its proximity to lived experience, yet emphasizes continuity over any rupture with tradition. Thus in the new comic fiction "an adventurer is levelled with the rest of the world, and acts in such scenes of the universal drama, as may be the lot of any other man" (cited in Williams 1970: 144), but Johnson still recognizes him as an adventurer, analogous to the hero of earlier, heroic, romance.

Conversely, in an influential essay on the "new species of writing" that appeared shortly after Johnson's piece, romance and novel are lumped together as the "old" writing, while the new, for the most part, goes nameless (the author occasionally refers to it as "biography" or "history"):

Sometime before this new Species of Writing appear'd, the World had been pester'd with Volumes, commonly known by the Name of Romances, or Novels, Tales, &c. fill'd with any thing which the wildest imagination could suggest. In all these Works, Probability was not required: The more extravagant the Thought, the more exquisite the Entertainment. Diamond Palaces, flying Horses, brazen Towers, &c. were here look'd upon as proper, and in Taste. In short, the most finish'd Piece of this kind, was nothing but Chaos and Incoherency. France first gave Birth to this strange Monster, and *England* was proud to import it among the rest of her Neighbour's Follies. A Deluge of Impossibility overflow'd the Press. Nothing was receiv'd with any kind of Applause, that did not appear under the Title of a Romance, or Novel; and Common

Sense was kick'd out of Doors to make Room for marvellous Dullness. The Stile in all these Performances was to be equal to the Subject – amazing: And may be call'd with great Propriety, "Prose run mad." This obtain'd a long Time. Every Beau was an *Oorondates*, and all the Belles were *Statiras*. Not a *Billet-doux* but run in Heroics, or the most common Message deliver'd but in the Sublime. The Disease became epidemical, but there were no Hopes of a Cure, 'till Mr. *Fielding* endeavour'd to show the World, that pure Nature could furnish out as agreeable Entertainment, as those airy non-entical Forms they had long ador'd, and persuaded the Ladies to leave this Extravagance to their *Abigails* with their cast Cloaths. Amongst which Order of People, it has ever since been observ'd to be peculiarly predominant."

(Anon. "An Essay on the New Species of Writing Founded by Mr. Fielding," 1751, cited in Williams 1970: 151)

The author notes the English debt to French prose, but only where the "old" writing is concerned. Moreover, though he initially notes that men, too, fashion themselves according to the dictates of French romance, he soon singles out female readers as in particular need of guidance from Mr Fielding and his new writing. Strikingly, the ostensible reformation of the weaker sex leads to the introduction of a class hierarchy: romances are cast off like old clothes, to be passed down to ladies' maids. The masculinization and exaltation of the new realism, whether or not it goes by the name of *novel*, is in full swing.

Interestingly, in Clara Reeve's *The Progress of Romance* (1785), a literary history couched as a series of dialogues, a woman takes up the defense of romance, both as author and as the character Euphrasia, the most knowledgeable discussant and the one responsible for setting the intellectual agenda. Romance and novel are clearly distinguished, although Reeve's stated purpose, to "show how the modern Novel sprung up out of [romance's] ruins" (Reeve 1930: 8), suggests a continuity. Reeve's larger project is fascinating: she attempts to rehabilitate romance by tracing the *longue durée* of a form that in her own time is particularly reviled. She identifies romance in the classical world and in the Middle Ages, as well as in the more proximate French heroic romances, and notes how texts classed as romances are often condemned for traits they share with other, highly regarded forms:

> Euph.: It is astonishing that men of sense, and of learning, should so strongly imbibe prejudices, and be so loth to part with them. That they should despise and ridicule Romances, as the most contemptible of all kinds of writing, and yet expatiate in raptures, on the beauties of the fables of the old classic Poets, on stories far more wild and extravagant, and infinitely more incredible.

> (Reeve 1930: 21)

Romance and novel, she admits, are often confused:

> Euph.: The word novel in all languages signifies something new. It was first used to distinguish these works from Romance, though they have lately been confounded together and are frequently mistaken for each other . . . The Romance is an heroic fable, which treats of fabulous persons and things. The Novel is a picture of real life and manners, and of the times in which it is written. The Romance in lofty and elevated language, describes what never happened nor is likely to happen. The Novel gives a familiar relation of such things, as pass every day before our eyes, such as may happen to our friend, or to ourselves; and the perfection of it, is to represent every scene, in so easy and natural a manner, and to make them appear so probable, as to deceive us into a persuasion (at least while we are reading) that all is real, until we are affected by the joys or distresses of the persons in the story, as if they were our own.

> (Reeve 1930: 110–11)

Despite Reeve's careful distinction between categories, general usage seems to conflate them more often than not. Thus the Earl of Chesterfield (1740–1?, pub. 1774) focuses on length as the primary distinguishing criterion: "A Novel is a kind of abbreviation of a Romance; for a Romance generally consists of twelve volumes, all filled with insipid love nonsense, and most incredible adventures" (cited in Williams 1970: 100). Yet he uses the term romance for both older fiction, "stuft with enchantments, magicians, giants, and such sort of impossibilities" and the newer sort, "within the bounds of possibility but not of probability" (cited in Williams 1970: 101).

In a 1787 essay in *The Microcosm*, George Canning adduces a "family likeness" between the two categories, with the novel as "the younger sister of Romance." The critic first pays lip service to what, by 1787, have become the hallmarks of the imperfect distinction between novel and romance:

> The fiction of romance is restricted by no fetters of reason, or of truth; but gives a loose to lawless imagination, and transgresses at will the bounds of time and place, of nature and possibility. The fiction of the other, on the contrary, is shackled with a thousand restraints; is checked in her most rapid progress by the barriers of reason; and bounded in her most excursive flights by the limits of probability.
>
> To drop our metaphors: we shall not indeed find in novels, as in romances the hero sighing respectfully at the feet of his mistress, during a ten years' courtship in a wilderness; nor shall we be entertained with the history of such a tour, as that of Saint George; who mounts his horse one morning at Cappadocia, takes his way through Mesopotamia, then turns to the right into Illyria, and so, by way of Grecia and Thracia, arrives in the afternoon in England. To such glorious violations as these of time and place, romance writers have an exclusive claim. Novelists usually find it more convenient to change the scene of courtship from a desert to a drawing-room . . .

Yet just when the reader becomes convinced of the differences between romance and novel, Canning notes the structural similarity that underlies surface distinctions: both forms are organized around a hero on a frustrated quest:

> But, these peculiarities of absurdity alone excepted, we shall find, that the novel is but a more modern modification of the same ingredients which constitute the romance; and that a recipe for the one may be equally serviceable for the composition of the other.
>
> A Romance (generally speaking) consists of a number of strange events, with a hero in the middle of them; who, being an adventurous knight, wades through them to one grand design, namely, the emancipation of some captive princess, from the oppression of a merciless giant; for the accomplishment of which purpose he must set at nought the incantations of the caitiff magician; must scale the ramparts of his castle; and baffle the vigilance of the female dragon, to whose custody his heroine is committed.

> Foreign as they may at first sight seem from the purposes of a novel, we shall find, upon a little examination, that these are in fact the very circumstances upon which the generality of them are built; modernized indeed in some degree, by the transformations of merciless giants into austere guardians, and of she-dragons into maiden aunts. We must be contented also that the heroine, though retaining her tenderness, be divested of her royalty; and in the hero we must give up the knight-errant for the accomplished fine gentleman.
>
> (Canning 1787, cited in Williams 1970: 341–2)

Canning recognizes in the novel many of the same narrative strategies and topoi that characterize the maligned older form. His witty transformation of "she-dragons into maiden aunts" invokes the same comedy that Johnson identified in the "new romance," indeed, one might even propose a certain ironic distance vis-à-vis the common structuring principles of the narrative as the true hallmark of the newer fiction. This ironic identification underlies, for example, Jane Austen's tongue-in-cheek name for the uxorious hero of *Emma* (1815): he is none other than Mr Knightley.

Yet beyond the confusion of terms which characterizes so much of the criticism surveyed above, there is an undeniable hybridization between older and newer forms of fiction in the late seventeenth and the eighteenth centuries. This melding is recognized by critics at the time. Reeve, for example, describes Delarivier Manley's oeuvre as "work that partakes of the style of the Romance, and the Novel" (Reeve 1930: 119). She is more explicit about the dual nature of Defoe's *Robinson Crusoe*, which "give[s] account of unknown or rather of *Ideal* countries, but in so natural and probable a manner, that [it] carries the reader with [it] wherever [it] please[s], in the midst of the most extraordinary occurrences" (Reeve 1930: 125). *Crusoe* thus challenges all existing categories; as Reeve's mouthpiece, Euphrasia, concludes: it partakes of both novel and romance, and constitutes "a different species from either . . . singular and Original" (Reeve 1930: 127).

Modern critics also recognize the ways in which romance makes its appearance in texts that no longer seem to fit a generic definition of romance: what one might call a "survival" of romance or, as I have suggested here, a version of romance as strategy. Aphra Behn's *Oroonoko* (1688), to take one signal example, clearly trades on many of the conventions of the heroic romance, to the extent that one critic calls it "one of the first and best examples of a heroic romance in miniature" (McDermott 1989: 128). Both hero and heroine are marked by the relentless idealization characteristic of the genre. The African prince Oroonoko has "that real Greatness of Soul, those refined notions of true Honour, that absolute Generosity, and that Softness that was capable of the highest Passions of Love and Gallantry," which the author suspects stems at least in part from "the Care of a French-Man of Wit and Learning" (Behn 1997: 12). His beloved Imoinda, for her part, is "the beautiful Black Venus to our young Mars" (Behn 1997: 14). The first part of the novella takes place in a highly stylized, Orientalist version of Africa, which invokes many of the clichés of the exotic found in heroic romances. The structure initially mimics the Greek romance, with faithful lovers divided by endless adventures and a heroine plagued with unwanted attentions, and culminates in their both being separated and sold into slavery.

Yet when the action follows the desperate Oroonoko (who believes Imoinda to be dead) to Surinam, the narrative changes radically. Here, the evidentiary register becomes crucial, as the author insists on her firsthand witnessing and participation in events. While this New World narrative is not realistic in any straightforward sense, neither does it idealize experience. In fact, it confronts the violence of Oroonoko's rebellion against his master, his murder of the pregnant Imoinda to save her from further slavery, and his attempt at self-destruction. Strikingly, when the violence becomes too much, it is not quietly elided, as it might be in an idealizing narrative; instead the narrator removes herself from what she cannot bear to witness: "the Sight [of Oroonoko] was gashly [ghastly], his Discourse was sad, and the earthly Smell about him so strong, that I was perswaded to leave the Place for some time" (Behn 1997: 64). Despite the narrator's inability to confront Oroonoko's destruction first-hand, the text embraces an almost naturalistic violence that contrasts powerfully with romance idealization.

Yet it would be simplistic to divide *Oroonoko* into an African heroic romance and an American chronicle; clearly part of Behn's point here is to harness the sympathies of romance and bring them to bear on the more ruthlessly historical part of her text. Thus romance functions here as a generic trace, a strategy that allows the narrative to invoke specific contexts and responses, most importantly the unwavering sympathy that heroic protagonists command. This makes the violence of the second part even more jarring, and forces the reader to consider how the representation of slavery changes radically when placed in a different generic context, one whose urgent sympathies belie the distance of more factual narratives.

There is a different survival of romance in *Pamela, or Virtue Rewarded* (1740–2), Samuel Richardson's wildly popular epistolary novel. A central example of the "new writing," *Pamela* describes the travails of a young maidservant who resists ardent pursuit by her master, the rakish Mr B, until she can persuade him to marry her. What this simple description cannot capture is how the interest of the narrative lies precisely in the breathless, even prurient deferral of the seduction: we read avidly of Pamela's confinement, her near rapes, her close escapes from the voracious sexual appetite of her master. At the most basic level, the structure of *Pamela* depends on the same kind of romance deferral as Heliodorus' *Ethiopica*, in which Chariclea's virtue is endlessly and miraculously preserved so that she can move on to the next trial. In both cases, delay is the great engine of narrative interest, and basically produces the text.

Pamela also resembles more proximate predecessors, typically classed as romances. Both title and subtitle echo these, in that the heroine's name as title was typical of passionate romance, while the subtitle recalls specific works: *Vertue Rewarded; or, The Irish Princess* (1693), and *The Surprize: or Constancy Rewarded* (1724) (McDermott 1989: 150). As Richetti has argued, it is possible to trace strong continuities between the fiction of the early and mid-eighteenth century, despite critical pronouncements to the contrary. Richetti finds the connection primarily in "an emotional (both erotic and pathetic) intensity inherent in the myth of persecuted innocence" (Richetti 1969: 169) that the texts offer their readers. This intensity, and the narrative deferral that produces it, can readily be identified as a romance strategy, linking the earlier texts commonly classed as passionate romances to the ostensibly new writing. In *Pamela*, as McDermott ably shows, both hero and heroine are conscious of their debt to these generic predecessors, styling their behaviors respectively after the rake and the resisting, chaste martyr (McDermott 1989: 151–2). Mr B complains to Pamela's father about the young woman's imaginative self-construction:

> I never knew so much romantic invention as she is mistress of. In short, the girl's head's turned by romances, and such idle stuff, to which she has given herself up, ever since her kind lady's death. And she assumes airs, as if she was a mirror of perfection, and every body had a design upon her.
>
> (Richardson 1980: 124)

But in fact Mr B himself uses romance to frame his advances on Pamela's virtue, attempting to transform her from would-be martyr into a willing literary accomplice of the right genre. Pamela's letter to her mother describes the first near-rape thus:

> May I, said I, Lucretia like, justify myself with my death, if I am used barbarously! Oh, my good girl, said he tauntingly, you are well read, I see; and we shall make out between us, before we have done; a pretty story in romance, I warrant ye.
>
> (Richardson 1980: 65)

Yet this knowingness about romance predecessors by no means cancels out the text's actual debt to romance; if anything, it drives home how impossible it is fully to separate novel and romance in the period. In *Pamela*, romance becomes strategic in multiple ways: it allows Richardson to tap into his readers' longstanding expectations and predilections, and to sustain narrative interest, while also providing ready-made scripts for the protagonists, who can then reflect on their own position vis-à-vis the tradition. While Richardson's text often appears to view romance from an ironic distance, it nonetheless depends on those same romance strategies. It is only a fully parodic rendering, such as Fielding's *Shamela* (1741) that reveals the full extent of *Pamela*'s debt.

Charlotte Lennox's *The Female Quixote* (1752) parodies the general fascination with romance, while also suggesting how it can provide a powerful antidote to reality, if not realism. Lennox's protagonist, Arabella, is a young lady brought up in such isolation from society that her principal experience of love and lovers comes from the heroic romances that she voraciously consumes. At one level, *The Female Quixote*, like its Cervantine precedent and the French anti-romances, parodies the powerful effects of popular romances on unsophisticated readers: Arabella expects the world to conform to her pet fictions, and spends much of the text making a fool of herself. Yet, much like *Don Quijote*, *The Female Quixote* may also be read as a far more complex account of the appeal of heroic fictions, given the social limitations on individual agency. Thus Lennox's Arabella brandishes the impossible standards of chastity and honor to which the protagonists of heroic romance are held as a defense against the prosaic matches planned by her father for a country heiress. As Doody suggests, Arabella finds in romance the possibility of an agency that is otherwise denied her (Lennox 1989: xxi–xxiii). Like Pamela, whose identification with romance heroines allows her to adopt a posture of inflexible resistance, Arabella uses romance to delay, if not fully to transform, her domestic fate.

Arabella attempts to educate her cousin, Mr Granville, who is also her suitor, by having him read the heroic romances "from which all useful Knowledge may be drawn; which give us the most shining Examples of Generosity, Courage, Virtue, and Love; which regulate our Actions, form our Manners, and inspire us with a noble Desire of emulating those great, heroic, and virtuous actions, which made those Persons so glorious in their Age, and worthy Imitation" (Lennox 1989: 48). Despite Arabella's confidence in the exemplary value of the romances, Granville cannot bring himself to read them, and the tension between her heroic view of the world and his own more prosaic one animates the narrative. Yet it is with some regret that we read of Arabella's ultimate disenchantment, at the hand of a clergyman, probably modeled on the figure of Dr Johnson, who convinces her that the romances are absurd and dangerous fictions:

> It is the Fault of the best Fictions, that they teach young Minds to expect strange Adventures and sudden Vicissitudes, and therefore encourage them often to trust to Chance. A long Life may be passed without a single Occurrence that can cause much Surprize, or produce any unexpected Consequence of great Importance; the Order of the World is so established, that all human Affairs proceed in a regular Method, and very little Opportunity is left for Sallies or Hazards, for Assault or Rescue; but the Brave and the Coward, the Sprightly and the Dull, suffer themselves to be carried alike down the Stream of Custom.
>
> (Lennox 1989: 379)

Though irrefutable, the clergyman's arguments are rather dispiriting; abandoning oneself to the "Stream of Custom" does not seem so preferable to escapism. He also fails to recognize the different forces that custom exercises over men and women. Surely the latter are far more hampered in their agency, given the parameters of this ordered world. Finally, the clergyman's appeal also ignores how Arabella's departure from custom actually improves her: though she is melodramatic and self-aggrandizing, she is also far more charitable and serious than the ladies whom she meets once she enters society, and has no concept of gossip, envy, or scandal. Thus despite the rebuke to which heroic romance is subjected, Lennox manages to suggest that the escapism of popular fiction can also protect the subject from the worst ravages of "Custom."

One way to make sense of the nostalgia for the values of heroic romance is to juxtapose it to the increasing concern over the incredible popularity of the new novels, with their relatively "familiar" plots and locations. Often these were deemed even more dangerous for young people than the old romances, precisely because of the realism that was so frequently praised. Here, moralistic condemnation seems to depend largely on the works' popularity: as novels supplant the heroic romances in the affections of readers, especially women and young people, they are declared more dangerous, and lower, than romances. Consider the following comparison, from 1778:

> If it be true, that the present age is more corrupt than the preceeding, the great multiplication of Novels has probably contributed to its degeneracy. Fifty years ago there was scarcely a Novel in the kingdom. Romances, indeed, abounded; but they, it is supposed, were rather favourable to virtue . . .
>
> That Richardson's Novels are written with the purest intentions of promoting virtue, none can deny. But in the accomplishment of this purpose scenes are laid open, which it would be safer to conceal, and sentiments excited, which it would be more advantageous to early virtue not to admit.
>
> (Vicesimus Knox, "On Novel Reading," cited in Williams 1970: 304)

Verisimilitude, it seems, does not necessarily make for the most uplifting or exemplary texts. Another critic, writing very soon after the publication of *The Female Quixote*, argues that it is preferable for young people to imitate the inimitable romances, à la Arabella, than to conduct themselves in a "natural" fashion:

> The writers of heroic romance, or the *Loves of Philodoxus and Urania*, professedly soar *above nature*. They introduce into their descriptions trees, water, air, &c. like common mortals; but then all their rivers are clearer than crystal, and every breeze is impregnated with the spices of Arabia. The manners of their personages seem full as extraordinary to our gross ideas. We are apt to suspect the virtue of two young people who are rapturously in love with each other, and who travel whole years in one another's company; though we are expressly told, that at the close of every evening when they retire to rest, the hero leans his head against a knotted oak, whilst the heroine seeks the friendly shelter of a distant myrtle. This, I say, seems to us a little unnatural; however, it is not of dangerous example. There can no harm follow if unexperienced persons should endeavor to imitate what may be thought inimitable. Should our virgins arrive but half way towards the chastity of a Parthenia, it will be something gained . . .
>
> (William Whitehead, *The World*, May 10, 1753, cited in Williams 1970: 207, emphasis in original)

Thus, paradoxically, the idealizing heroic romance finds itself favorably compared to the new writing. As the general taste turns from the artifice of the former to the relative realism of the latter, moralists deplore the dangers of fictions that are too close to real experience. The nostalgia does not extend to other forms of romance, but only to the highly overwrought and explicitly moralizing fictions of Scudéry and her fellows. As we shall see, romance as a more general category continues to be associated with the fictions read by an increasingly broad public, as in the highly popular fictions known as "gothic romances," and, predictably, once again criticized as a dangerous influence.

ROMANCING THE GOTHIC

By the mid-eighteenth century, literary scholars in Germany, France, and England were reacting to the dictates of neoclassicism, questioning its privileging of reason, order, and proportion. The gradual construction of a "Gothic" tradition to counter the classical legacy of Greece and Rome involved a rediscovery of the literary heritage of the Middle Ages and Renaissance, which had largely been neglected in favor of the classics. In the narrow sense, "Gothic" referred primarily to the production of ancient Northern Europeans, the Goths or barbarians who had opposed Rome with their own traditions of liberty and social organization. More broadly, the Gothic designated everything that was not classical: both the vernacular works of the Middle Ages, and those Renaissance texts that eschewed the "rediscovered" classical heritage in favor of "native" traditions. Given the deep engagement of medieval romance with its classical antecedents, and the mixed allegiances of Ariosto, Tasso, and Spenser, this kind of distinction seems to us deeply problematic. Yet for eighteenth-century critics such as Richard Hurd, Thomas Percy, and Thomas Warton, neglected romance, broadly construed to include everything from ballads to chivalric tales, presented an alternative to the classical and a rich source for a native literary tradition.

For Hurd, the rehabilitation of the Gothic required proving that chivalric romance, in particular, reflected the reality of an age, and presented its own kind of logic. In his *Letters on Chivalry and Romance* (1762), Hurd provides an extended comparison between "Greek and Gothic times" (Hurd 1963: 26–38 and passim). Although comparing the ostracized culture to the gold standard of Greece seems to undermine Hurd's claims to relativism, the exercise is an attempt to prove that the productions of a chivalric age are as heroic, and thus as worthy, as Greek epic poetry. Hurd revisits the old Italian quarrels over Ariosto and Tasso, reminding his readers that although the Italians themselves now value their tradition, the fashion for French neoclassicism has led to its neglect elsewhere (79–81). More importantly, in an English context the French fashion has deprived Spenser of his rightful place, and exalted truth over fancy: "What we have gotten by this revolution, you will say, is a great deal of good sense. What we have lost, is a world of fine fabling" (120).

But Hurd's project goes beyond antiquarianism and the recovery of the past. He also prescribes a new set of rules to replace Aristotelian neoclassicism. Not all poetry, he insists, must obey "the trite maxim of *following nature*" (93, emphasis in original). While realism has its place in poetry on "men and manners," the more "sublime and creative poetry

. . . addressing itself solely or principally to the Imagination," need not observe the same "cautious rules of credibility" (94–5). Instead, Hurd exalts "fancies . . . not only more gallant, but, on a change of the scene, more sublime, more terrible, more alarming, than those of the classic fablers" (54–5). Thus, not only is the Gothic recuperated, it surpasses the classical in its direct address to the imagination, becoming the poetic wellspring par excellence.

Two important developments in the history of romance follow the Gothic revival that Hurd advocates, although in both cases the causal connections are far from straightforward, and (as usual) the terminology is vexing. First, the last decades of the eighteenth century see the introduction of a distinct new genre that quickly achieves great popularity: the Gothic romance, which self-consciously revives "medieval" motifs in often sensational tales. Second, the privileging of the imagination over reason, and thus the revindication of romance forms, becomes one of the hallmarks of the movement we now know as Romanticism. As both the Gothic and Romanticism are explored in separate volumes in this series, I will not give an extended account of either here, but will simply position them vis-à-vis the larger problem of romance.

GOTHIC AS GENRE

From its beginnings, the Gothic romance, or novel, is explicitly presented as a mixture of new and old. The genre is self-consciously inaugurated by Horace Walpole, with *The Castle of Otranto* (1764), a fantastically popular tale that has appeared in over 100 editions since its first publication. Sir Walter Scott, in his introduction to the Edinburgh edition of 1811, praises it as "the first modern attempt to found a tale of amusing fiction upon the basis of the ancient romances of chivalry" (cited in Walpole 1964: viii). *Otranto* establishes some of the most enduring conventions of the genre: ancient castles complete with secret vaults and passageways; family secrets; obscure prophecies; ghosts and apparitions; hidden identities. More importantly, it exacerbates the narrative tension attendant on what Richetti calls "persecuted innocence," a constant among various forms of popular narrative in the eighteenth century, which in this case involves an innocent princess pursued by the lascivious and immoral father of the prince she was to wed.

But whereas early novels such as *Pamela* owe an unacknowledged debt to romance, the Gothic self-consciously looks back, combining modern skepticism with an appreciation of the emotional and aesthetic effects of the marvelous. Walpole's two prefaces are characterized by their knowingness about literary fashion. The preface to the first edition, in which he pretends to be the translator of an obscure text – a venerable strategy since Chrétien and Cervantes – sets the tone for the Gothic as dark and medieval, yet nonetheless refined:

> The following work was found in the library of an ancient catholic family in the north of England. It was printed at Naples, in the black letter, in the year 1529. How much sooner it was written does not appear. The principal incidents are such as were believed in the darkest ages of christianity; but the language and conduct have nothing that favours of barbarism. The style is the purest Italian.
>
> (Walpole 1964: 3)

The "translator" then attempts to situate the text in a Counter-Reformation context, as an example of ancient superstitions cynically promoted:

> Letters were then in their most flourishing state in Italy, and contributed to dispel the empire of superstition, at that time so forcibly attacked by the reformers. It is not unlikely that an artful priest might endeavour to turn their own arms on the innovators; and might avail himself of his abilities as an author to confirm the populace in their ancient errors of superstitions.
>
> (3)

This hypothetical priest, then, uses the narrative to "enslave a hundred vulgar minds." Yet in the reader's own day such strategies are clearly obsolete. Instead, the translator claims, the text "can only be laid before the public at present as a matter of entertainment" (4), and apologetically at that:

> Even as such, some apology for it is necessary. Miracles, visions, necromancy, dreams, and other preternatural events, are exploded now even from romances . . . Belief in every kind of prodigy was so established in those dark ages, that an author would not be faithful to

the *manners* of the times who should omit all mention of them. He is not bound to believe them himself, but he must represent his actors as believing them.

(4, emphasis in original)

The preface recontextualizes the romance marvelous as historically appropriate, and no longer a dangerous fraud. The modern reader, like the author, will not be taken in by it, but should nonetheless appreciate its accuracy. Beyond this "*air* of the *miraculous*" (4, emphasis in original), the "translator" insists, the text is perfectly natural: "Allow the possibility of the facts, and all the actors comport themselves as persons would do in their situation" (4). In the preface to the second edition, where Walpole drops his pretense of translation, he is explicit about his "attempt to blend the two kinds of romance, the ancient and the modern":

In the former, all was imagination and improbability: in the latter, nature is always intended to be, and sometimes has been, copied with success. Invention has not been wanting; but the great resources of fancy have been damned up, by a strict adherence to common life . . . The author of the following pages thought it possible to reconcile the two kinds. Desirous of leaving the powers of fancy at liberty to expatiate through the boundless realms of invention, and thence of creating more interesting situations, he wished to conduct the mortal agents in his drama according to the rules of probability; in short, to make them think, speak, and act, as it might be supposed mere men and women would do in extraordinary positions.

(7–8)

Yet despite Walpole's emphasis on nature, and the rationality attributed to his contemporary audience, what makes the Gothic so popular is precisely its gallery of marvelous and otherworldly topoi. In fact, although early imitators of Walpole, such as Clara Reeve, repeat his proclaimed goal of combining "the most attractive and interesting circumstances of the ancient romance and modern novel" (Reeve, *The Old English Baron* [1778], cited in Walpole 1964: vii), the genre soon becomes associated with the most fantastical elements of the romance tradition.

These "well-wrought scenes of artificial terror which are formed by a sublime and vigorous imagination," critics conjectured, provided a particular kind of pleasure, in which the imagination "rejoices in the expansion of its powers," so that "the pain of terror is lost in amazement" (John and Anna Laetitia Aikin, "On the Pleasure Derived from Objects of Terror" [1773], cited in Williams 1970: 284–5). Because these topoi were clearly what attracted readers to the genre, authors turned to them repeatedly, soon rendering them trite conventions. This connection between the striking popularity of the Gothic and its iterability suggests how the category of romance continues its modern fall from "high" to "low," becoming increasingly associated with mass or genre literature. I discuss this at greater length in the last section of this chapter, but must first turn to the connection between romance and Romanticism.

ROMANCE AND ROMANTICISM

The complicated connections between romance and Romanticism lead to much confusion in our current terminology. As the OED confirms, there is still considerable ambiguity in usage. The signal opposition between *romantic* and *classical*, developed by German critic A.W. Schlegel in the early nineteenth century, was echoed and disseminated by Madame de Staël's *De l'Allemagne* (1813) in both France and England, and by Samuel Taylor Coleridge's contemporary lectures. These authors all participated in the new privileging of the romantic, as the organic wellspring of imagination and feeling, over the neoclassical. The first references to the movement that we now know as Romanticism regularly associate it with *romance*, in the sense of the idealized Gothic and chivalric past promoted in an earlier generation by Hurd and his contemporaries. At the same time, however, there is an emerging awareness of Romanticism as a distinct movement, so that the adjective *Romantic* comes to refer to a specific school of art, literature, and music.

Yet what does literary Romanticism have to do with romance, in the many senses we have explored here? While Romanticism revives and recirculates many of the topoi associated particularly with medieval romance, such as the marvelous, the magical, the mysterious, it does not engage it in the precise instantiations we have encountered. In fact, Romanticism is not particularly interested in romance as narrative strategy or form, much less as a translation of classical originals into national vernaculars. Instead, it privileges a certain nostalgic purchase on times gone by, idealizing what it imagines as the organic culture of a romance past, and its seductive appeal. Thus in *The Prelude* William Wordsworth uses the notion of romance to characterize the heady, early days of the French Revolution:

> Bliss was it in that dawn to be alive,
> But to be young was very Heaven! O times,
> In which the meagre, stale, forbidding ways
> Of custom, law, and statute, took at once
> The attraction of a country in romance!
> When Reason seemed the most to assert her rights
> When most intent on making of herself
> A prime enchantress – to assist the work,
> Which then was going forward in her name!
> (Wordsworth 1979: 11.108–16)

The transformation of Reason into a romance enchantress describes for the poet the particular appeal of the Revolution's impossible idealism, now conclusively lost. John Keats, for his part, begins his sonnet "On Sitting Down to Read King Lear Once Again" with another conflicted acknowledgement of the charm of romance: "O golden-tongued Romance, with serene Lute!/ Fair plumed Syren, Queen of far-away!" Romance beguiles these poets even when they know better, luring them towards an irretrievable past.

As Rita Copeland has pointed out, this kind of "archaic idealism . . . constructs a myth of the Middle Ages and thus a myth of its own origins and recuperative enterprise" (Copeland 1991: 222). Copeland suggests that romance, in this sense, becomes a metonymic stand-in for "a Middle Ages viewed by turns as chivalrous, sentimental, childish, and most of all, archaic" (220), a far cry, she points out, from the literary modernity that romance as an operation actually signified in the time of Chrétien. The relation of nineteenth-century Romantics with romance, one might surmise, is analogous to that of nineteenth-century medievalism with the Middle Ages: while interesting cultural phenomena in their own right, they have relatively little to do with any precise meaning the latter might have had in their original contexts. Thus, while it would certainly be possible, and perhaps even fruitful, to trace the transformation of romance topoi in Romanticism, the conflation of the categories seems only to create more confusion. I would therefore like to suggest that we reserve the adjective *romantic* – capitalized or not – for discussions of the influential nineteenth-century school, and that we use *romance*, as both noun and adjective, to refer the much broader topic of this book.

ROMANCE AND "GENRE LITERATURE"

If we consider "mass" or "genre" literature as popular writing based on a successful formula that can be endlessly repeated, it is easy to see how such forms might relate to the more complex meanings of romance that I have analyzed here. Northrop Frye readily identifies the close connections between romance and contemporary popular forms, as well as the "curiously proletarian status" of romance (Frye 1976: 23). In this section, I examine the identification of romance with texts generally derided as genre literature through what are variously known as "Harlequin romances" or "romance novels," as well as through other forms less commonly connected to the romance tradition.

Harlequin romances take their name from the fantastically successful publishing house that has become synonymous with the form. The North American company, and its British subsidiary, Mills & Boon, dominate the paperback romance market across the English-speaking world. As Harlequin/Silhouette or Harlequin Mills & Boon, the publishers employ hundreds of writers to produce a steady supply of "series" or "category" titles, providing eager readers with monthly doses of their preferred genre. The books are also available as longer, stand-alone titles. Their popularity, in sheer numbers, is astounding: according to the writers' association Romance Writers of America (RWA), romance titles make up more than half of all sales in popular paperback fiction, and generate over U\$S 1 billion per year in sales in North America alone. RWA identifies two central criteria that define a romance for the association:

> A Central Love Story – In a romance, the main plot concerns two people falling in love and struggling to make the relationship work. The conflict in the book centers on the love story. The climax in the book resolves the love story. A writer is welcome to as many subplots as she likes as long as the relationship conflict is the main story.

> An Emotionally Satisfying and Optimistic Ending – Romance novels
> end in a way that makes the reader feel good. Romance novels are based
> on the idea of an innate emotional justice – the notion that good people
> in the world are rewarded and evil people are punished. In a romance,
> the lovers who risk and struggle for each other and their relationship are
> rewarded with emotional justice and unconditional love.
>
> (http://www.rwanational.org/romance.stm)

RWA also specifies a handful of subgenres, from the more traditional historical romances, which construct a fanciful historical setting for the love story, to the more recent developments such as the hugely popular "suspense romance" or the "time-travel romance."

Yet why are these narratives known as romances in the first place? Although they certainly fit the fifth OED definition of "That class of literature which consists of romances; romantic fiction. spec. a love story; that class of literature which consists of love stories," they appear to have little in common with Greek, chivalric, or heroic romance. Yet in certain ways the romance novels bring together several strands of the romance tradition we have analyzed: they are often characterized by a nostalgic vision of the past, a relentlessly idealizing tone, and an emphasis on the female sphere, from a female protagonist to a view of the world organized around love.

Although the RWA definition fails to specify it, the female heroine is of central importance, as is the authorial voice implied in the association's assumption of a female writer. Men may well write romance novels pseudonymously, but they must be published under female names. In Pedro Almodóvar's fondly ironic film version of the world of romance writers, *The Flower of My Secret* (1996), a hugely popular writer dismays her publishing house when she announces that she wants to write a "serious" novel instead of her usual predictable fare. A devoted fan saves the day by stepping in to ventriloquize her writing. The catch, of course, is that he is a man. His apparent success in the impersonation gently questions the exclusive femininity of the romance-novel world and underscores the formulaic nature of the writing.

For, like chivalric romances, romance novels are remarkably iterable: their familiarity, as variations on a basic narrative, is a large part of what makes them so appealing to readers. Janice Radway suggests that the romance novels function for their readers "as the ritualistic repetition of a single, immutable cultural myth" (Radway 1984: 198), reassuring them with their limited variation on a well-known theme. The main narrative strategy is the postponement of the union between the lovers. Unlike the Greek version, however, in which the two are separated by outside obstacles after they recognize their love for each other, romance novels focus primarily on the heroine's gradual, often reluctant, realization of her love for a superficially antagonistic hero. The largely internalized dilemma of her recognition of her own feelings replaces the externalized threats of pirates and bandits.

When feminist or Marxist scholars address the romance novel, their verdict is overwhelmingly negative. Reading beyond the surface structure of the happy ending in a wedding, actual or anticipated, they argue that the heroine's happiness is achieved only by sacrificing her independence and succumbing to the dictates of a patriarchal society. Certain critics nonetheless emphasize the productive distance between the reader and the heroine: far from identifying with the innocent yet rebellious heroine in mindless ways, the reader is confronted with the distance between the utopian view of marriage in the romance and her own everyday existence (Modleski 1980: 448). In a survey of Mills & Boon romances from the mid-1980s, Ann Rosalind Jones detects an increasing, though vexed, engagement with feminism, for "none [of the texts] can work out a seamless fit between the claims of modern women and the old rib-bones of romance" (Jones 1986: 204). The apparently positive treatment of feminism, Jones suggests, may herald an updating of the genre's sexual politics; less sanguinely, it might simply "indicate editorial confidence that the genre can absorb enough feminism to appeal to a changing readership while still containing the movement's radical potentials" (Jones 1986: 211). A more recent anthology of romance writers' responses to criticism suggests that while heroines may be older and involved in a wide range of professions, any departure from the dangerous, intractable hero is profoundly unpersuasive to readers (Clair 1992: 70–1). Novelist Jayne Ann Krentz is uncompromising:

> The effort to make romance novels respectable has been a resounding failure. The books that exemplify the "new breed" of politically correct romances, the ones featuring sensitive, unaggressive heroes and sexually

> experienced, right-thinking heroines in "modern" stories dealing with
> trendy issues, have never become the most popular books in the genre.
>
> (Krentz 1992b: 113)

Krentz suggests that readers value precisely the atavistic, archetypal aspects of romance that are most troubling to feminist critics.

In an effort to transcend external hierarchies of value, critics such as Radway adopt an ethnographic approach, focusing on how romance readers themselves understand the role of the texts in their lives (Radway 1984: 9 and passim). Yet even this sympathetic critic concludes that:

> while the act of romance reading is used by women as a means of partial
> protest against the role prescribed for them by the culture, the discourse
> itself actively insists on the desirability, naturalness, and benefits of that
> role by portraying it not as the imposed necessity that it is but as a freely
> designed, personally controlled, individual choice.
>
> (Radway 1984: 208)

Defenders of romance novels attempt to counter these powerful readings by emphasizing the similarity between the genre, in the contemporary mass-market sense, and earlier novels equally concerned with courtship and marriage. Pamela Regis argues that such canonical novels as *Pamela*, *Sense and Sensibility*, and *Jane Eyre* are essentially romance novels, and that the merits of the contemporary versions are unfairly overlooked by both academic critics and the media (Regis 2003: 53–5, and passim; see also Clair).

Clearly, amatory romance and its successors, as well as the gothic romance, were early avatars of the contemporary romance novel. It is also evident that individual works may well transcend the limitations of genre and formula. Yet Regis' attempt to redefine the genre as a whole, particularly by invoking illustrious predecessors, ignores the limitations of the romance novels' formulaic construction. Beyond the actual recipes provided by publishers to would-be authors, the texts deliberately curtail both their vocabulary and the range of their descriptions:

> [D]espite important differences, the Regency, the gothic, the historical,
> and the contemporary all characterize their romantic heroes as

> "passionate," "hard," "mocking," "indifferent," "moody," "masculine," "magnetic," "fierce," "ruthless," and "overbearing." Marked redundancy and intertextual repetition are characteristic of romantic fiction. Such a recurring vocabulary inevitably creates stock descriptions and formulaic characterizations that reconfirm reader expectations over and over again.
>
> (Radway 1984: 195–6)

In a sense, what so many critics deplore is exactly what the readers appreciate: both groups know exactly what they will find when they turn to romance novels. As romance novelists Linda Barlow and Krentz argue in their defense of the genre, the conventional language does not indicate their limitations as writers, but is instead part of their deliberate coded understanding with readers:

> [The reader] is reminded of this tacit contract every time she picks up a book, reads the back cover copy, and registers such code phrases as "a lust for vengeance," "a hunter stalking his prey," "marriage of convenience," "teach the devil to love." Drawing on her own emotional and intellectual background, both inside and outside the romance genre, she responds to these code phrases with lively interest and anticipation as she looks forward to the pleasurable reading experience the novel promises.
>
> (Barlow and Krentz 1992: 18)

As these writers confirm, despite devoted readers' determination to find the most satisfying romances, as evinced in Radway's study, they seek *representative* examples of their own privileged formula.

It is important to remember that the romance novel, strikingly marginalized in critical discourse despite its popularity, is not the only contemporary genre fiction to utilize romance strategies. Science fiction, fantasy, spy stories, the Western, and a host of other genres also feature an idealizing quest narrative that often pits the hero against society, and in which his progress is continuously undone by obstacles and delays. All are iterable and predictable: John Cawelti, in a ground-breaking study of genre fiction, identifies them as "formula stories" (Cawelti 1976). It is striking, therefore, that romance novels in particular are explicitly associated with romance, given their feminization of experience and their relegation to a place at the very bottom of the literary hierarchy. As Regis notes, even the devotees of romance novels, unlike fans of science fiction or adventure stories, feel the need to disguise their reading preferences in public (Regis 2003: xi). (In some cases, publishers or book clubs provide handy false covers to place over the bodice-ripper art.) Thus even within the larger category of mass-market genre fiction, the term romance marks the most criticized and also least recognized kind, the one associated with young or infantilized female readers and particularly deplored.

Yet these romance forms are only marginal in some ways. Not only are they immensely popular with readers, they also inform the "high" culture with which they are often unthinkingly contrasted. Although critics might not have much respect for contemporary avatars of romance, certain highly regarded novelists, for example, have found them fruitful material. Popular, mass-market versions of romance often furnish content or ironic form for novelists interested precisely in the undying appeal of their formulas. Such varied texts as Manuel Puig's *Heartbreak Tango* (1981), Mario Vargas Llosa's *Aunt Julia and the Scriptwriter* (1982), and John Fowles' *The French Lieutenant's Woman* (1969) invoke the conventions of genre literature and examine the powerful fantasies it provides for those who consume it. Implicitly, all these texts question the artificiality of boundaries between "high" and mass-market literature, even as they involve the self-regarding reader in the voyeurism, prurience, and, indeed, simple delight of the texts. They often portray the disillusion that stems from the fundamental divergence between ideal and reality, a behind-the-scenes look that is not often afforded by genre literature itself. Other writers, such as A.S. Byatt, playfully foreground the category of romance, appealing to the longer tradition that lies behind the novel. Byatt's *Possession* (1990), a sophisticated, highly self-conscious love-story about literary critics pursuing romance in its various forms, bears the simple subtitle *A Romance*. Romance also makes its appearance in contemporary fiction's embrace of the marvelous, often referred to as "magical realism." These explicit challenges to the purported realism of the novel suggest that the simple dichotomy between realist novel and non-realist romance is no longer valid, assuming it ever was.

Romance often transcends the written form. Strategies of delay and deferral, iteration, variations on a basic formula, and idealization are clearly at work in television's situation comedies and soap operas, and in

Hollywood film. Individual works often take up romance topoi, but beyond the topical connections there are important similarities in the way of telling a story. The elements that some critics find so depressingly predictable, such as the gloss, the happy ending, the limited depiction of a world where wealth itself is idealized, suggest how visual representations, too, can favor a formulaic idealization. Of course, film can also reflect on this dynamic: in Neil La Bute's *Nurse Betty* (2000), a young woman escapes unspeakable violence by retreating into a fantasy soap-opera universe. Her quest takes her from Kansas to Los Angeles, to seek out the "doctor" she admires in her favorite hospital melodrama. Though reality fails to conform to her expectations, she perseveres in her quixotic attempts to seek refuge in the idealized on-screen world manufactured by the studios, with often hilarious results.

Perhaps, then, the attempt to circumscribe romance to popular or to "high" forms is fundamentally misguided. In its broadest, most abstract form, romance functions as a cluster of narrative strategies that can be employed with greater or lesser degrees of self-consciousness to produce genre-effects in both high and low narratives. Although we can identify certain recurrent traits – such as delay and deferral, the pleasure of the reader, a fascination with female vulnerability, an emphasis on the marvelous over the quotidian, a focus on the travails of the individual, a nostalgia for other times and places – the flexibility of romance suggests that it will continue to appear in new forms, rendering any definition necessarily provisional. One might even argue that romance as strategy exceeds the bounds of literary or artistic creation, to animate, say, political narratives of idealization and deferral. What seems certain is that romance is hardly superseded by the novel; indeed, the teleological model of the progress of narrative appears, from this perspective, all too simplistic. Instead, despite its frequent demotion in literary hierarchies, romance remains an essential critical idiom, an indispensable tool for understanding the power of narrative to captivate and enchant.

FURTHER READING

Bakhtin, M. M. (1981) *The Dialogic Imagination: Four Essays*, trans. Caryl Emerson and Michael Holquist, Austin: University of Texas Press.
[Early and influential theory includes earlier works in an expanded definition of the novel; especially telling, though largely negative, account of the Greek romances.]

Brownlee, Kevin and Marina Scordilis Brownlee (eds.) (1985) *Romance: Generic Transformation from Chrétien de Troyes to Cervantes*, Hanover: University Press of New England.
[Excellent anthology on medieval and Renaissance forms of romance.]

Cawelti, John G. (1976) *Adventure, Mystery and Romance: Formula Stories as Art and Popular Culture*, Chicago: University of Chicago Press.
[One of the first, and most important, considerations of "genre literature."]

Doody, Margaret Anne (1996) *The True Story of the Novel*, New Brunswick, NJ: Rutgers University Press.
[Key argument about the marginalization of romance in literary history; emphasizes continuities between earlier forms and the later novel.]

Frye, Northrop (1957) *Anatomy of Criticism*, Princeton, NJ: Princeton University Press.
[Central structuralist theory of romance as enduring mode.]

—— (1976) *The Secular Scripture: A Study of the Structure of Romance*, Cambridge, MA: Harvard University Press.
[Expanded transhistorical consideration of romance as the "structural core of all fiction."]

Krueger, Roberta L. (ed.) (2000) *The Cambridge Companion to Medieval Romance*, Cambridge: Cambridge University Press.
[Essential anthology by some of the most influential contemporary scholars of medieval romance; serves both as an introduction and as a sophisticated guide to further study.]

Jameson, Frederic (1981) "Magical Narratives: On the Dialectical Use of Genre Criticism," in *The Political Unconscious: Narrative as a Socially Symbolic Act*, Ithaca, NY: Cornell University Press.
[Central Marxist argument for reading genre – in this case, medieval romance – in its historical context and as a "social contract" between writers and readers.]

McDermott, Hubert (1989) *Novel and Romance: The Odyssey to Tom Jones*, Totowa, NJ: Barnes & Noble.

[A transhistorical introduction to the "continuum" of narrative modes in fiction.]

Parker, Patricia A. (1979) *Inescapable Romance: Studies in the Poetics of a Mode*, Princeton, NJ: Princeton University Press.
[Groundbreaking deconstructive and transhistorical study of the way romance functions within texts, with an emphasis on the Renaissance.]

Radway, Janice (1984) *Reading the Romance: Women, Patriarchy, and Popular Literature*, Chapel Hill: University of North Carolina Press.
[Important study of modern romance novels and their readers, based on an ethnographic model.]

Reardon, Bryan P. (1991) *The Form of Greek Romance*. Princeton, NJ: Princeton University Press.
[Excellent introduction to romance in the classical world.]

Tatum, James (ed.) (1994) *The Search for the Ancient Novel*, Baltimore, MD: Johns Hopkins University Press.
[Essential anthology on "ancient fiction," including both theoretical discussions and connections to later periods.]

Weinberg, Bernard (1961) *A History of Literary Criticism in the Italian Renaissance*, 2 vols., Chicago: University of Chicago Press.
[Exhaustive survey of Renaissance theories and literary quarrels about romance, especially in the second volume.]

Williams, Ioan M. (1970) *Novel and Romance, 1700–1800: A Documentary Record*, New York: Barnes & Noble.
[Essential anthology of eighteenth-century criticism on the two categories, collected from prefaces, periodicals, letters, etc.]

SELECT BIBLIOGRAPHY

Apollonius King of Tyre (1989) trans. Gerald N. Sandy in Bryan P. Reardon (ed.), *Collected Ancient Greek Novels*, Berkeley: University of California Press.

Apuleius (1993) *The Transformations of Lucius Otherwise Known as The Golden Ass*, trans. Robert Graves, New York: Noonday Press.

Archibald, Elizabeth (1991) *Apollonius of Tyre: Medieval and Renaissance Themes and Variations: Including the Text of the Historia Apollonii Regis Tyri with an English Translation*, Rochester, NY: Boydell & Brewer.

Ariosto, Ludovico (1974) *Orlando Furioso*, trans. Guido Waldman, New York: Oxford University Press.

Aucassin and Nicolette and Other Mediaeval Romances and Legends, (1951) trans. Eugene Mason, London: J. M. Dent., Princeton, NJ: Princeton University Press.

Auerbach, Eric (1953) *Mimesis: The Representation of Reality in Western Literature*, trans. Willard R. Trask, Princeton, NJ: Princeton University Press.

Austen, Jane (1971) *Emma*, David Lodge (ed.), London: Oxford University Press.

Baker, Herschel (ed.) (1971) *Four Essays on Romance*, Cambridge, MA: Harvard University Press.

Bakhtin, M. M. (1981) *The Dialogic Imagination: Four Essays*, trans. Caryl Emerson and Michael Holquist, Austin: University of Texas Press.

Barlow, Linda, and Krentz, Jayne Ann (1992) "Beneath the Surface: The Hidden Codes of Romance," in Jayne Ann Krentz (ed.), *Dangerous Men & Adventurous Women: Romance Writers on the Appeal of the Romance*, Philadelphia: University of Pennsylvania Press.

Barron, W. R. J. (1987) *English Medieval Romance*, New York: Longman.

Baswell, Christopher (2000) "Marvels of Translation and Crises of Transition in the Romances of Antiquity," in Roberta L. Krueger (ed.), *The Cambridge Companion to Medieval Romance*, Cambridge: Cambridge University Press.

Beaton, Roderick (1996) *The Medieval Greek Romance*, New York: Routledge.

Beer, Gillian (1970) *The Romance*, London: Methuen.

Behn, Aphra (1997) *Oroonoko*, Joanna Lipking (ed.), New York: W.W. Norton.

Benoît de Sainte-Maure (1987) *Le Roman de Troie*, trans. Emmanuèle Baumgartner, Paris: Union Générale d'Éditions.

Boiardo, Matteo Maria (1978) *Orlando Innamorato*, Giuseppe Anceschi (ed.), Milan: Garzanti.

Brownlee, Kevin and Brownlee, Marina Scordilis (eds.) (1985) *Romance: Generic Transformation from Chrétien de Troyes to Cervantes*, Hanover: University Press of New England.

Bruckner, Matilda Tomaryn (2000) "The Shape of Romance in Medieval France," in Roberta L. Krueger (ed.), *The Cambridge Companion to Medieval Romance*, Cambridge: Cambridge University Press.

Byatt, A. S. (1990) *Possession: A Romance*, London: Chatto & Windus.

Cascardi, Anthony J. (2002) "Don Quixote and the Invention of the Novel," in Anthony J. Cascardi (ed.), *The Cambridge Companion to Cervantes*, Cambridge: Cambridge University Press.

Cavafy, C. P. (1992) *Collected Poems*, revised edition, trans. Edmund Keeley and Philip Sherrard, George Savidis (ed.), Princeton, NJ: Princeton University Press.

Cawelti, John G. (1976) *Adventure, Mystery and Romance: Formula Stories as Art and Popular Culture*, Chicago: University of Chicago Press.

Cazelles, Brigitte (ed.) (1991) *The Lady as Saint: A Collection of French Hagiographic Romances of the Thirteenth Century*, Philadelphia: University of Pennsylvania Press.

Cervantes Saavedra, Miguel de (1992) *Exemplary Novels / Novelas ejemplares*, B.W. Ife (ed.), Warminster, England: Aris & Phillips.

—— (1995) *Don Quijote*, trans. Burton Raffel, New York: W.W. Norton.

Chariton (1989) *Chaereas and Callirhoe*, trans. Bryan P. Reardon, in Bryan P. Reardon (ed.), *Collected Ancient Greek Novels*, Berkeley: University of California Press.

Chaucer, Geoffrey (1989) *The Canterbury Tales: Nine Tales and the General Prologue*, V. A. Kolve and Glending Olson (eds.), New York: W.W. Norton.

—— (1998) *Troilus and Criseyde: A New Translation*, trans. Barry Windeatt, Oxford: Oxford University Press.

Chrétien de Troyes (1991) *Arthurian Romances*, trans. with intro. and notes William W. Kibler, London: Penguin.

Clair, Daphne (1992) "Sweet Subversions," in Jayne Ann Krentz (ed.), *Dangerous Men & Adventurous Women: Romance Writers on the Appeal of the Romance*, Philadelphia: University of Pennsylvania Press.

Coleridge, Samuel Taylor (1959) *Writings on Shakespeare: A Selection of the Essays, Notes, and Lectures of Samuel Taylor Coleridge on the Poems and Plays of Shakespeare*, Terence Hawkes (ed.), New York: Capricorn Books.

Columbus, Christopher (1961) *Four Voyages to the New World: Letters and Selected Documents*, trans. and ed. R.H. Major, New York: Corinth Books.

Congreve, William (1970) "Preface to *Incognita*, 1691," in Ioan Williams (ed.), *Novel and Romance 1700–1800: A Documentary Record*, New York: Barnes & Noble.

Copeland, Rita (1991) "Between Romans and Romantics," *Texas Studies in Literature and Language* 33.2: 215–24.

Danson, Lawrence (2000) *Shakespeare's Dramatic Genres*, Oxford: Oxford University Press.

Dante (1980) *The Divine Comedy. Vol. 1: Inferno*, trans. Allen Mandelbaum, Berkeley: University of California Press.

Davis, Lennard J. (1996) *Factual Fictions: The Origins of the English Novel*, Philadelphia: University of Pennsylvania Press.

Day, Geoffrey (1987) *From Fiction to the Novel*, New York: Routledge.

De Armas, Frederick A. (2002) "Cervantes and the Italian Renaissance," in Anthony J. Cascardi (ed.), *The Cambridge Companion to Cervantes*, Cambridge: Cambridge University Press.

Di Piero, Thomas (1992) *Dangerous Truths and Criminal Passions: The Evolution of the French Novel, 1569–1791*, Stanford, CA: Stanford University Press.

Díaz del Castillo, Bernal (1963) *The Conquest of New Spain*, trans. J. M. Cohen, London: Penguin.

Doody, Margaret Anne (1996) *The True Story of the Novel*, New Brunswick, NJ: Rutgers University Press.

Dowden, Edward (1879) *Shakspeare*, New York: Appleton.

Dragonetti, Roger (1980) *La Vie de la lettre au moyen âge (le conte du Graal)*, Paris: Éditions du Seuil.

D'Urfé, Honoré (1995) *Astrea, Part 1*, trans. and intro. Steven Rendall, Binghamton, NY: Medieval and Renaissance Texts and Studies.

Eisenberg, Daniel (1982) *Romances of Chivalry in the Spanish Golden Age*, Newark, NJ: Juan de la Cuesta.

Eneas: A Twelfth-Century French Romance (1974) trans. with intro. and notes John A. Yunck, New York: Columbia University Press.

Ercilla, Alonso de (1993) *La Araucana*, Isaías Lerner (ed.), Madrid: Cátedra.

Field, Rosalind (ed.) (1999) *Tradition and Transformation in Medieval Romance*, Rochester, NY: D.S. Brewer.

Fisher, Sheila (2000) "Women and Men in Late Medieval English Romance," in Roberta L. Krueger (ed.), *The Cambridge Companion to Medieval Romance*, Cambridge: Cambridge University Press.

Flores, Angel (ed.) (1957) *Masterpieces of the Spanish Golden Age*, New York: Holt, Rinehart and Winston.

The Flower of My Secret (1996) dir. Pedro Almodóvar.

Foucault, Michel (1973) *The Order of Things: An Archaeology of the Human Sciences*, New York: Pantheon.

Fowles, John (1969) *The French Lieutenant's Woman*, Boston: Little, Brown and Co.

Frye, Northrop (1957) *Anatomy of Criticism*, Princeton, NJ: Princeton University Press.

—— (1976) *The Secular Scripture: A Study of the Structure of Romance*, Cambridge, MA: Harvard University Press.

Fuchs, Barbara (2001) *Mimesis and Empire: The New World, Islam, and European Identities*, Cambridge: Cambridge University Press.

—— (2003) *Passing for Spain: Cervantes and the Fictions of Identity*, Chicago: University of Illinois Press.

Gaunt, Simon (2000) "Romance and Other Genres," in Roberta L. Krueger (ed.) *The Cambridge Companion to Medieval Romance*, Cambridge: Cambridge University Press.

Geoffrey of Monmouth (1991) *Historia Regum Britannie*, ed. and trans. Neil Wright, Cambridge: D.S. Brewer.

Gesner, Carol (1970) *Shakespeare and the Greek Romance*, Lexington: University of Kentucky Press.

Giamatti, A. Bartlett (1966) *The Earthly Paradise and the Renaissance Epic*, Princeton, NJ: Princeton University Press.

Goldberg, Jonathan (1981) *Endlesse Worke: Spenser and the Structures of Discourse*, Baltimore, MD: Johns Hopkins University Press.

Goodman, Jennifer R. (1998) *Chivalry and Exploration, 1298–1630*, Woodbridge, Suffolk: The Boydell Press.

Greene, Robert (1957) *Pandosto*, in *The Descent of Euphues, Three Elizabethan Romance Stories: Euphues, Pandosto, Piers Plainness*, Cambridge: Cambridge University Press.

Greene, Thomas (1963) *The Descent from Heaven: A Study in Epic Continuity*, New Haven, CT: Yale University Press.

—— (1982) *The Light in Troy: Imitation and Discovery in Renaissance Poetry*, New Haven, CT: Yale University Press.

Hampton, Timothy (1990) *Writing from History: The Rhetoric of Exemplarity in Renaissance Literature*, Ithaca, NY: Cornell University Press.

Harth, Erica (1983) *Ideology and Culture in Seventeenth-Century France*, Ithaca, NY: Cornell University Press.

Heiserman, Arthur Ray (1977) *The Novel Before the Novel: Essays and Discussions About the Beginnings of Prose Fiction in the West*, Chicago: University of Chicago Press.

Heldris de Cornuälle (1972) *Le Roman de Silence: A Thirteenth-Century Arthurian Verse-Romance*, Lewis Torpe (ed.), Cambridge: Heffer.

Heliodorus (1989) *An Ethiopian Story*, trans. J. R. Morgan, in Bryan P. Reardon (ed.), *Collected Ancient Greek Novels*, Berkeley: University of California Press.

Heng, Geraldine (1992) "A Woman Wants: The Lady, *Gawain*, and the Forms of Seduction," *The Yale Journal of Criticism* 5.3: 101–33.

—— (1998) "Cannibalism, the First Crusade, and the Genesis of Medieval Romance," *Differences*, 10.1: 98–174.

—— (2003) *Empire of Magic: Medieval Romance and the Politics of Cultural Fantasy*, New York: Columbia University Press.

Hexter, Ralph J. (1993) *A Guide to the Odyssey: A Commentary on the English Translation of Robert Fitzgerald*, New York: Vintage Books.

Hollier, Denis (ed.) (1989) *A New History of French Literature*, Cambridge, MA: Harvard University Press.

Homer (1998) *Odyssey*, trans. Robert Fitzgerald, New York: Farrar, Straus, and Giroux.

Huet, Pierre-Daniel (1942) *Traité de l'origine des romans*, Arend Kok (ed.), Amsterdam: N.V. Swets & Zeitlinger.

Hunter, J. Paul (1990) *Before Novels: The Cultural Contexts of Eighteenth-Century English Fiction*, New York: W.W. Norton.

Huot, Sylvia (2000) "The Manuscript Content of Medieval Romance," in Roberta L. Krueger (ed.) *The Cambridge Companion to Medieval Romance*, Cambridge: Cambridge University Press.

Hurd, Richard (1963) *Letters on Chivalry and Romance* (1762) Hoyt Trowbridge (ed.), Los Angeles: William Andrews Clark Memorial Library, University of California.

Jameson, Frederic (1975) "Magical Narratives: Romance as Genre," *New Literary History* 7: 135–63.

—— (1981) "Magical Narratives: On the Dialectical Use of Genre Criticism," in *The Political Unconscious: Narrative as a Socially Symbolic Act*, Ithaca, NY: Cornell University Press.

Johnson, Carroll (2001) *Cervantes and the Material World*, Chicago: University of Illinois Press.

Johnston, Arthur (1964) *Enchanted Ground: The Study of Medieval Romance in the Eighteenth Century*, London: Athlone Press.

Jones, Ann Rosalind (1986) "Mills & Boon Meets Feminism," in Jean Radford (ed.), *The Progress of Romance: The Politics of Popular Fiction*, London: Routledge.

Kay, Sarah (1995) *The* Chansons de Geste *in the Age of Romance: Political Fictions*, Oxford: Clarendon Press.

—— (1997) "Who Was Chrétien de Troyes?" in James P. Carley and Felicity Riddy (eds.), *Arthurian Literature XV*, Cambridge: D.S. Brewer.

—— (2000) "Courts, Clerks and Courtly Love," in Roberta L. Krueger (ed.) *The Cambridge Companion to Medieval Romance*, Cambridge: Cambridge University Press.

Keats, John (1978) *The Poems of John Keats*, Jack Stillinger (ed.), Cambridge, MA: Harvard University Press.

Ker, W. P. (1908) *Epic and Romance: Essays on Medieval Literature*, London: Macmillan.

Kern, Edith (1968) "The Romance of Novel/Novella," in Peter Demetz, Thomas Greene, and Lowry Nelson Jr. (eds.), *The Disciplines of Criticism: Essays in Literary Theory, Interpretation, and History*, New Haven, CT: Yale University Press.

Konstan, David (1994) *Sexual Symmetry: Love in the Ancient Novel and Related Genres*, Princeton, NJ: Princeton University Press.

Krentz, Jayne Ann (ed.) (1992a) *Dangerous Men and Adventurous Women: Romance Writers on the Appeal of the Romance*, Philadelphia: University of Pennsylvania Press.

—— (1992b) "Trying to Tame the Romance: Critics and Correctness," in Jayne Ann Krentz (ed.), *Dangerous Men and Adventurous Women: Romance Writers on the Appeal of the Romance*, Philadelphia: University of Pennsylvania Press.

Krueger, Roberta L. (ed. and intro.) (2000) *The Cambridge Companion to Medieval Romance*, Cambridge: Cambridge University Press.

Le Roman de Thèbes (The Story of Thebes) (1986) trans. John Smartt Coley, New York: Garland Publishing.

Lennox, Charlotte (1989) *The Female Quixote, or, The Adventures of Arabella*, Margaret Dalziel (ed.), Margaret Doody (intro.), London: Oxford University Press.

Leonard, Irving (1992) *Books of the Brave*, 2nd edition, Berkeley: University of California Press.

Longus (1989) *Daphnis and Chloe*, trans. Christopher Gill, in Bryan P. Reardon (ed.), *Collected Ancient Greek Novels*, Berkeley: University of California Press.

McDermott, Hubert (1989) *Novel and Romance: The Odyssey to Tom Jones*, Totowa, NJ: Barnes & Noble.

McKeon, Michael (1987) *The Origins of the English Novel, 1600–1740*, Baltimore, MD: Johns Hopkins University Press.

McMurran, Mary Helen (2002) "National or Transnational? The Eighteenth-Century Novel," in Margaret Cohen and Carolyn Dever (eds.), *The Literary Channel: The International Invention of the Novel*, Princeton, NJ: Princeton University Press.

Malkin, Irad (1998) *The Returns of Odysseus: Colonization and Ethnicity*, Berkeley: University of California Press.

Malory, Sir Thomas (1977) *Works of Malory*, Eugène Vinaver (ed.), Oxford: Oxford University Press.

—— (1998) *Le Morte D'Arthur: The Winchester Manuscript*, Helen Cooper (ed., with intro. and notes), Oxford: Oxford University Press.

Marie de France (1999) *The Lais of Marie de France*, 2nd edition, trans. Glen S. Burgess and Keith Busby, London: Penguin.

Martorell, Joanot (1984) *Tirant lo Blanc*, trans. David H. Rosenthal, New York: Schocken Books.

Menocal, Maria Rosa (1987) *The Arabic Role in Medieval Literary History: A Forgotten Heritage*, Philadelphia: University of Pennsylvania Press.

Milton, John (2000) *Paradise Lost*, John Leonard (ed.), New York: Penguin.

Modleski, Tania (1980) "The Disappearing Act: A Study of Harlequin Romances," in *Signs: Journal of Women in Culture and Society* 5.3: 435–48.

Murnaghan, Sheila (1987) *Disguise and Recognition in the Odyssey*, Princeton, NJ: Princeton University Press.

Nerlich, Michael (1987) *Ideology of Adventure: Studies in Modern Consciousness, 1100–1750*, trans. Ruth Crowley, Minneapolis: University of Minnesota Press.

Newcomb, Lori Humphrey (2002) *Reading Popular Romance in Early Modern England*, New York: Columbia University Press.

Nolan, Barbara A. (1992) *Chaucer and the Tradition of the Roman Antique*, Cambridge: Cambridge University Press.

Nurse Betty (2000) dir. Neil La Bute.

Ovid (2001) *The Metamorphoses of Ovid*, trans. Michael Simpson, Amherst: University of Massachusetts.

—— (2002) *The Art of Love*, bilingual edition, trans. James Michie, New York: Modern Library.

Parker, Patricia A. (1979) *Inescapable Romance: Studies in the Poetics of a Mode*, Princeton, NJ: Princeton University Press.

—— (1990) "Romance," in A. C. Hamilton (ed.), *The Spenser Encyclopedia*, Buffalo: University of Toronto Press.

Perkins, Judith (1999) "An Ancient 'Passing' Novel: Heliodorus' Aithiopika," *Arethusa* 32: 197–214.

Perry, B. E. (1967) *The Ancient Romances: A Literary-Historical Account of their Origins*, Berkeley: University of California Press.

Petrarch, Francesco (1976) *Petrarch's Lyric Poems: The Rime sparse and Other Lyrics*, trans. Robert Durling, Cambridge, MA: Harvard University Press.

Pettet, E. C. (1949) *Shakespeare and the Romance Tradition*, London: Staples.

Pope, Alexander (1940) *The Rape of the Lock and Other Poems*, Geoffrey Tillotson (ed.), London: Methuen.

Puig, Manuel (1981) *Heartbreak Tango: A Serial*, trans. Suzanne Jill Levine, New York: Vintage.

Quint, David (1985) "The Boat of Romance and Renaissance Epic," in Kevin Brownlee and Marina Scordilis Brownlee (eds.), *Romance: Generic Transformation from Chrétien de Troyes to Cervantes*, Hanover: University Press of New England.

—— (1993) *Epic and Empire: Politics and Generic Form from Virgil to Milton*, Princeton, NJ: Princeton University Press.

Radway, Janice (1984) *Reading the Romance: Women, Patriarchy, and Popular Literature*, Chapel Hill: University of North Carolina Press.

Reardon, Bryan P. (ed.) (1989) *Collected Ancient Greek Novels*, Berkeley: University of California Press.

—— (1991) *The Form of Greek Romance*. Princeton, NJ: Princeton University Press.

Reeve, Clara (1930) *The Progress of Romance and The History of Charoba, Queen of Aegypt: Reproduced from the Colchester edition of 1785*, New York: Facsimile Text Society.

Regis, Pamela (2003) *A Natural History of the Romance Novel*, Philadelphia: University of Philadelphia Press.

Rhu, Lawrence F. (1993) *The Genesis of Tasso's Narrative Theory: English Translations of the Early Poetics and a Comparative Study of their Significance*, Detroit: Wayne State University Press.

Richardson, Samuel (1980) *Pamela*, Fielding, Henry, *Shamela*, New York: Meridian Classic.

Richetti, John J. (1969) *Popular Fiction before Richardson: Narrative Patterns 1700–1739*, Oxford: Clarendon Press.

Riley, E. C. (1964) *Cervantes' Theory of the Novel*, London: Oxford University Press.

Rodríguez de Montalvo, Garci (1857) *Las sergas de Esplandián*, Pascual de Gayargos (ed.), Madrid: M. Rivadeneyra.

—— (1974) *Amadís of Gaul*, trans. Edwin B. Place and Herbert C. Behm, 2 vols, Lexington: University of Kentucky Press.

Romance Writers of America (website) http://www.rwanational.org.

Scott, Sir Walter (1887) *Essays on Chivalry, Romance, and the Drama*, London: Frederick Warne.

Segre, Cesare (1985) "What Bakhtin Left Unsaid: The Case of the Medieval Romance," in Kevin Brownlee and Marina Scordilis Brownlee (eds.), *Romance: Generic Transformation from Chrétien de Troyes to Cervantes*, Hanover: University Press of New England.

Shakespeare, William (1988) *The Late Romances: Pericles, Cymbeline, The Winters Tale, The Tempest*, David Bevington (ed.), New York: Bantam.

Sidney, Philip (1983) *Arcadia*, 2 vols., Delmar, NY: Scholars' Facsimiles & Reprints.

Sieber, Harry (1985) "The Romance of Chivalry in Spain: From Rodríguez de Montalvo to Cervantes," in Kevin Brownlee and Marina Scordilis Brownlee (eds.), *Romance: Generic Transformation from Chrétien de Troyes to Cervantes*, Hanover: University Press of New England.

Sir Gawain and the Green Knight (1983) trans. Keith Harrison, London: Folio Society.

Spenser, Edmund (1978) *The Faerie Queene*, Thomas P. Roche (ed.), New York: Penguin.

Spitzer, Leo (1948) *Linguistics and Literary History: Essays in Stylistics*, Princeton, NJ: Princeton University Press.

Spufford, Margaret (1981) *Small Books and Pleasant Histories: Popular Fiction and its Readership in Seventeenth-Century England*, Athens: University of Georgia Press.

Stephens, Susan A. and Winkler, John J. (eds.) (1995) *Ancient Greek Novels: The Fragments*, Princeton, NJ: Princeton University Press.

Stevens, John E. (1973) *Medieval Romance: Themes and Approaches*, London: Hutchinson.

Tasso, Torquato (1973) *Discourses on the Heroic Poem*, trans. Mariella Cavalchini and Irene Samuel, Oxford: Clarendon Press.

—— (1987) *Jerusalem Delivered*, trans. Ralph Nash, Detroit: Wayne State University Press.

Tatius, Achilles (1989) *Leucippe and Clitophon*, trans. John J. Winkler, in Bryan P. Reardon (ed.), *Collected Ancient Greek Novels*, Berkeley: University of California Press.

Tatum, James (ed.) (1994) *The Search for the Ancient Novel*, Baltimore, MD: Johns Hopkins University Press.

Teresa de Avila (1991) *The Life of Teresa of Jesus: The Autobiography of Teresa of Ávila*, trans. E. Allison Peers, New York: Doubleday.

The Trojan War: The Chronicles of Dictys of Crete and Dares the Phrygian (1966) trans. R. M. Frazer Jr., Bloomington: Indiana University Press.

Tylus, Jane (1993) "Reasoning away Colonialism: Tasso and the Production of the *Gerusalemme liberata*," *South Central Review* 10.2: 100–14.

Vargas Llosa, Mario (1982) *Aunt Julia and the Scriptwriter*, trans. Helen R. Lane, New York: Farrar, Straus, Giroux.

Vinaver, Eugène (1971) *The Rise of Romance*, New York: Oxford University Press.

Virgil (1984) *Aeneid*, trans. Robert Fitzgerald, New York: Vintage Books.

Vives, Juan Luis (2000) *The Education of a Christian Woman: A Sixteenth-Century Manual*, Charles Fantazzi (ed. and trans.), Chicago: University of Chicago Press.

Vogeley, Nancy (2001) "How Chivalry Formed the Myth of California," *Modern Language Quarterly* 62.2: 165–87.

Wace (1999) *Wace's Roman de Brut: A History of the British: Text and Translation*, trans. Judith Weiss, Exeter: University of Exeter Press.

Walpole, Hugh (1964) *The Castle of Otranto: A Gothic Story*, W. S. Lewis (ed.), London: Oxford University Press.

Watt, Ian (1957) *The Rise of the Novel: Studies in Defoe, Richardson and Fielding*, Berkeley: University of California Press.

Weinberg, Bernard (1961) *A History of Literary Criticism in the Italian Renaissance*, 2 vols., Chicago: University of Chicago Press.

Williams, Ioan M. (1970) *Novel and Romance, 1700–1800: A Documentary Record*, New York: Barnes & Noble.

Wilson, Diana de Armas (2000) *Cervantes, the Novel, and the New World*, New York: Oxford University Press.

—— (2002) "Cervantes and the New World," in Anthony J. Cascardi (ed.), *The Cambridge Companion to Cervantes*, Cambridge: Cambridge University Press.

Winkler, John J. (1994) "The Invention of Romance," in James Tatum (ed.), *The Search for the Ancient Novel*, Baltimore, MD: Johns Hopkins University Press.

Winkler, John J. and Williams, Gordon (eds.) (1982) *Later Greek Literature*, Cambridge: Cambridge University Press.

Wordsworth, William (1979) *The Prelude 1799, 1805, 1850*, Jonathan Wordsworth, M. H. Abrams and Stephen Gill (eds.), New York: W.W. Norton.

Wroth, Mary (1995) *The First Part of The Countess of Montgomery's Urania*, Josephine A. Roberts (ed.), Binghamton, NY: Center for Medieval and Early Renaissance Studies, State University of New York at Binghamton.

—— (1999) *The Second Part of the Countess of Montgomery's Urania*, Josephine A. Roberts (ed.), Tempe, AZ: Renaissance English Text Society in conjunction with Arizona Center for Medieval and Renaissance Studies.

Xenophon of Ephesus (1989) *An Ephesian Tale*, trans. Graham Anderson, in Bryan P. Reardon (ed.), *Collected Ancient Greek Novels*, Berkeley: University of California Press.

Zumthor, Paul (1954) *Histoire littéraire de la France médiévale (VIe–XIVe siècles)*, Paris: Presses Universitaires de France.

INDEX